3.00.

THE MOORHOUSE I. X. MILLAR LECTURE SERIES

PROSPERITY WITHOUT INFLATION • NUMBER ONE • *1957*
ARTHUR F. BURNS

ECONOMIC PLANNING IN UNDERDEVELOPED AREAS
NUMBER TWO • *1958*
EDWARD S. MASON

A PROGRAM FOR MONETARY STABILITY
NUMBER THREE • *1959*
MILTON FRIEDMAN

THE KEYNESIAN SYSTEM • NUMBER FOUR • *1961*
DAVID MCCORD WRIGHT

THE STRATEGY OF ECONOMIC POLICY

RAYMOND J. SAULNIER

THE MILLAR LECTURES · NUMBER FIVE · 1962

FORDHAM UNIVERSITY PRESS · NEW YORK

© FORDHAM UNIVERSITY PRESS • 1963 • NEW YORK

LIBRARY OF CONGRESS CATALOG CARD NUMBER: 63–14408

Foreword

THE PROBLEMS OF ECONOMIC POLICY, aside from their technical complexity, are further complicated by the fact that such policies may interact with considerations lying outside the scope of economic analysis. Since economic processes and aims take place within a wider social context, solutions for purely economic problems bought at the price of unintended changes elsewhere in the total picture may prove to be ultimately too expensive. Thus *public* action, too, may turn out to involve, in an even more literal sense of the term, "social costs" of its own.

That this may be so in some general, unspecified sense is widely, but not universally, acknowledged. Some insist that social welfare can be measured by purely economic criteria alone—a view which one observer has characterized as "thoroughly metaphysical"; and which, one may add, could involve the fallacy of composition on a rather grand scale. But even general acceptance of some nebulous larger frame of reference is of little practical use without some exploration of its implications for economic strategy. And this implies that we be able to identify the "parameters"— so to speak—both economic and noneconomic, of the total society we want, and also to specify to what extent, if at all, these latter impose constraints on the range of choice of acceptable policy alternatives.

Surprisingly little has so far been accomplished along these lines by economists—possibly because we tend to confuse economics and its applications. Economic *theory* can claim—perfectly correctly—the privilege of a science to delimit provisionally its field of inquiry and to treat as "given" the excluded (i.e. noneconomic) considerations. But it is very doubtful that economic *practice,* including policy, can lay claim to the same privilege in view of the different arena in which it operates.

The recent resurgence of interest in "welfare" economics testifies to some concern with this problem. On the one hand, attempts to identify something like the "parameters" mentioned earlier are discernible in current discussions of social welfare "functions," "criteria," and "tests"—especially if we overlook the excessive preoccupation of these discussions with purely redistributive effects. On the other hand, theories about the nature and source of such parameters range all the way from the assertion that they originate from outside economics, whether in unspecified form or as a "value-consensus," to an "instrumentalism" which relates them to an evolving set of self-correcting value-judgments about welfare.

Contemporary theorizing about welfare, however, seems to fall short in at least two respects: the welfare "function" or "criterion" is dealt with only on a highly formal level largely devoid of empirical content; and there has been no convincing demonstration as to just how such a criterion, even if completely specified, would guide the choice among alternative economic policies. It is precisely in these respects, I think, that Professor Saulnier, in the latest series of Millar Lectures comprising the present volume, makes valuable contributions. One has only to read "social welfare function" for what Saulnier describes as our

national purpose to realize that here is a definite criterion or para-
meter ready for testing—and one which represents, it is reasonable to assume, a high degree of "value-consensus." Moreover, he
proceeds to draw from his experience and reflection to provide the
reader with a lucid object lesson in how to go about judging among
timely and controversial policy issues both according to tests of
consistency among themselves and, what is much more, within
the constraints set by our national social ideals.

LOUIS M. SPADARO
Professor of Economics

Department of Economics
Fordham University
April, 1963

Prefatory Note

THE FOUR CHAPTERS WHICH comprise this volume were delivered as the Moorhouse I. X. Millar Lectures in the fall of 1962 at Fordham University, at the invitation of the university's Department of Economics.

A good deal has happened since the lectures were given that bears on their subject matter and I have been sorely tempted to reflect some of these developments in them. But the temptation was resisted and except for revisions growing out of a struggle with one major structural problem and the usual fretting over language they appear here as they were given.

They can be summarized in a few words. The first chapter deals with what I fear is a neglected aspect of the strategy of economic policy, namely, how the policies we follow to achieve our strictly economic objectives—high and vigorously rising levels of production, employment and income—can affect the institutional framework of our society and, in so doing, can adversely affect our national purpose, which is to provide maximum opportunities for self-directed personal development.

The second states three related imperatives of economic

policy, to which strategy must defer: (1) anti-inflationism, which we must all respect; (2) a conservative federal budget, which it is in particular the responsibility of our federal government to prepare; and (3) a noninflationary wage policy, which in our democratic society it is the responsibility of the leadership of labor and business to find and to practice.

The third chapter examines, and rejects, a point of view rather popular nowadays to the effect that an "easy" fiscal policy implemented through generous increases in government spending or liberal tax reductions or both can be substituted for an "easy" money policy where the latter has been incapacitated, as it has been in the United States today, by an imbalance in international financial accounts.

Finally, in the fourth chapter I have suggested a strategy of policy which I think would serve us well in the present situation. Its major elements are: (1) rigorous expenditure control by the federal government; (2) modest tax reduction, which for budgetary reasons I would limit to the corporate profits tax and to the very high rates levied on the top and intermediate brackets of personal income and which I would try to legislate as soon as possible; (3) the limitation of advances in labor costs for the moment at least to amounts that are well within, rather than equal to, productivity improvements; and (4) a still more vigorous effort than any yet made to eliminate the deficit in our balance of international payments. As for tax reduction in the present context, I have argued that this must not be so planned as to enlarge the current deficit in our federal budget and I have made specific suggestions as to how tax reductions can be accomplished without this potentially harmful result.

Of course, this is far from the whole story of the strategy of economic policy, let alone the whole story of its tactical implementation. But I trust it will suffice to show that there is a positive, activist approach to current economic problems that is also a conservative approach. That is, I trust it will suffice to show that there is a way of going about these things that promises a lasting improvement of our economic performance and which, at the same time, will strengthen further the institutions of political and economic freedom which are our respected heritage and our best hope for the future.

I am deeply grateful for Fordham University's invitation to continue in these lectures what is already a distinguished series and particularly to Father William T. Hogan S.J., who extended the invitation in the first place and made the undertaking a most pleasant experience for me, and to Father Edwin A. Quain S.J., Director of the Fordham University Press, who has skillfully and patiently seen the volume to publication.

RAYMOND J. SAULNIER
Professor of Economics
Barnard College
Columbia University

March 4, 1963

Table of Contents

Foreword by Louis M. Spadaro   v

Prefatory Note   ix

Chapter One

National Purpose and the Strategy
  of Economic Policy   1

Chapter Two

Three Imperatives of Economic Policy   18

Chapter Three

Some Recent Lessons of Experience
  on the Use of Economic Policy Measures   38

Chapter Four

Essentials of a Strategy of Economic Policy   57

Chapter One

National Purpose and the
Strategy of Economic Policy

MY SUBJECT IN THESE FOUR CHAPTERS is the strategy of economic policy, but we cannot begin directly with the strictly economic aspect of these questions because we cannot, as I know you will agree, adequately define or design a strategy of economic policy without having in mind to begin with a clear concept of national purpose. By this I mean not merely a concept of what we are seeking to achieve in a strictly economic sense, though this is essential. What we need is a concept of the kind of world, or perhaps I should say the kind of society, in which we want to live. We need, of course, to know all we can about how the economic policies we choose to follow are affecting our national aspirations, and may affect them in the future. But to have a value judgment on such matters, to be able to say, that is, whether a given effect is good or bad, a clear understanding of paramount purpose is indispensable.

Yet a concept of national purpose is by no means always explicit in discussions of economic policy. More often than not it is merely taken for granted. Discourse on these matters typically tends to concentrate on narrowly economic objectives, and on short-run measures of economic performance, at that. Especially, it very often fails to take account of the bearing of what we do to achieve our economic objectives on the institutional framework of the world in which we live.

There is a grave danger in this. The danger is that our policy choices will alter the framework of our society in ways we would not deliberately choose. And because, as I shall argue, the institutional framework of our society is basic to the achievement of our national purpose, the inadvertent result of policy may be to frustrate that purpose.

We can be quite sure that our economic policy choices will affect the forms and structure of our society in one way or another; policy choices are rarely altogether neutral in this respect. But we cannot be sure that the impact will conform to our preferences. Certainly we can have little assurance on this critical point unless we are quite clear as to the kind of social organization we prefer, and as clear as we can be as to how it is likely to be affected by the strategy and tactics of our economic policies. This first chapter is addressed, accordingly, to the question of national purpose and to the bearing on our success in achieving national purpose of the efforts we make to reach our strictly economic goals.

The clue to our concept of national purpose is not hard to find; it lies in the fact that in our society the central interest is in the individual. Our highest goals are those that have to do with the development and fulfillment of the individual personality, and our paramount national purpose derives from this. To put it simply, our purpose is to provide the greatest possible opportunity for self-directed personal development and fulfillment consistent with the parallel rights of others. We may call this "responsible individualism." Our society's institutional framework, and in particular the framework of its economic institutions, has a crucial bearing on our success in achieving national purpose, so defined. That bearing is expressed in our belief that maximum opportunities for self-directed personal development are afforded in a society in which economic activity is carried out through the institutions of competitive, market-oriented enterprise, based on the institution of private property. And because economic policy affects the institutional framework of our society one way or another, it can make or break our effort to achieve that success.

Although this belief in the essentiality of an enterprise system for the maintenance of free institutions generally is the traditional view of the American people, it is, as we know very well, a point around which much controversy has centered. The most extreme objection to it, expressed in Marxist-Leninist doctrine, claims that the individual finds full opportunity for development only within the framework of essentially collectivist institutions. But the personal development in which we are interested is not development inspired and directed by a centralized, external power, as in the Soviet state. The essence of personal development as we wish it, in a free society, is self-direction.

It may be protested, as it often is, that the individual in our free society is not in fact free from external influences, and it would be an ill-starred venture to undertake completely to rebut this. However, there is no need to do so. It is not necessary to an appreciation of the values inherent in a free society to believe that in such a society the individual makes his decisions in a kind of institutional vacuum. To acknowledge the impact on ourselves of the world around us should not bar us from recognizing that there is maximum opportunity in the atmosphere of a free society based on the concept of responsible individualism, and within the framework of an enterprise economy, to direct one's affairs according to one's own lights. There need be no absence in such a society of arrangements to protect and advance the common interest, and to prevent the exercise of self-interest by one individual or group from unjustly intruding upon and harming the interests of others. The arrangements we have built into our society to provide these protections are far from perfect, to be sure, but they are remarkably good. And we are alert to their deficiencies and on the whole aggressive in our efforts to correct them.

As concerns the Marxist-Leninist protest and its claims, we are nowadays, fortunately, a good bit more discriminating than has been the case in the past. Whatever may be said of the ultimate opportunities for individual development within the collectivist society—and I have grave doubts as to these opportunities —the record shows clearly enough that these societies have made precious little progress to date in providing them, despite the fact that one such system, the Soviet Union, has had nearly half a century in which to do it. All that is necessary to sense the poverty of such opportunity in the collectivist society is to browse for a few minutes at the newsstand of any one of the cities of the Soviet Union. Not that to browse at our own magazine and bookracks is an altogether edifying experience, for it is far from that; but, even so, the comparison is enormously favorable to us.

It is precisely on this matter of the position of the individual in the society and of the individual's freedom that we place most store. It is instructive, for example, that our most deeply felt complaint against the collectivist system is its failure to respect the interest of the individual, as an individual, and its failure to allow opportunity for genuinely self-directed personal development. To remind ourselves of this reaction to the collectivist system should help to clarify our own concept of national purpose. It should strengthen our dedication to democratic ideals to realize that our fondest hope for the collectivist world is that it will in some manner, at some time, provide the scope and opportunities for self-directed personal development afforded by the democratic, individualistic society.

The ultimate test to which we put the collectivist system runs in terms of the scope of individual liberty which it can provide. Equally, this must be the ultimate and continuing test of our own society. And, thus, a strategy of economic policy acceptable to us must be one that promotes and strengthens free institutions.

*   *   *   *

On this understanding of national purpose, and on this understanding of how our economic institutions bear on our chances of achieving national purpose, let us consider more closely the character of our strictly economic objectives.

Clearly, our economy and our economic life contribute to national purpose not just by being an open system in which there are maximum opportunities for personal development, but also by helping to maximize, through the efficient use of resources, the individual's economic well-being. This is not to say that the economic factor is the only one bearing on man's well-being. Indeed, it is our rejection of such a view that distinguishes us from the materialists. It is merely to say that by providing for the economic facet of man's well-being our economy contributes to the enhancement of welfare in the fullest and broadest sense. And, of course, when we ask how our economy contributes to man's economic well-being the answer must be by performing efficiently in the production of goods and services for consumption, that is, in the production of goods and services that satisfy human needs and desires, including education, medical care, facilities for religious and cultural life, etc., as well as food, clothing, housing and the rest.

How could it be otherwise? The proposition that the purpose of our economy is to produce goods and services for human consumption would seem to be so obvious as to preclude serious debate and it is not easy to believe that consumption could be understood in anything but this inclusive sense. But apparently not so. Having stated once in the course of congressional hearings that ". . . as I understand an economy, its ultimate purpose is to produce more consumer goods . . ." and having stated this in a context that could leave no doubt in the mind of any reasonable and objective listener that this implied consumption in the broadest sense, I have been astonished to see the view repeatedly assailed. Perhaps the most amazing observation on the question, which oddly enough was made by an economist, is that appearing in a recent study which finds in this attribution of primacy to consumption the key to the difference in the economics of our two national political parties.[1] This is a remarkable interpretation, considering all that has been said over the years on the objectives of economic effort. It warrants asking the question: what could be the purpose of an economy if it is not to produce goods and services for human consumption?

It is true that over a period of time an increase in the output of investment or capital goods may contribute more to the growth

---

1. Seymour E. Harris, *The Economics of the Political Parties* (Macmillan, New York, 1962), p. 342–43. In passages that are absolutely stunning for their lack of objectivity, Professor Harris transforms a stated interest in "consumption" into an interest in nothing but "longer cars with larger fins, bigger refrigerators, more and more gadgets and gimmicks," and into a lack of concern for "adequate provision for resources development, for medical care, for housing, for social welfare."

Arthur M. Schlesinger, Jr. has addressed himself to the same point, employing language somewhat more lurid than that of Professor Harris. In *The Politics of Hope* (Houghton Mifflin Company, Boston, 1963), p. 83, he writes of the "contemporary orgy of consumer goods" and manages to read into the consumption goal a wish "not to produce better people or better schools or better health or better national defense or better opportunities for cultural and spiritual fulfillment—but to produce more gadgets and gimmicks to overwhelm our bodies and distract our minds." He continues, "As against what we self-righteously condemn as the godless materialism of the Communists we seem to have dedicated ourselves to a godly materialism of our own."

of the economy, and certainly to its capacity for future growth, than an equivalent increase in the output of goods for immediate consumption. But growth in itself is not our end-purpose, and ultimately the expansion of capital goods output is useful and desirable to the extent that it is reflected in some way in an improvement in economic well-being. Obviously, any thought that the objective of maximizing the production of goods for consumption precludes an interest in the output of capital goods must be rejected as devoid of any economic sense.

Nor is the consumption-goods objective to be interpreted as precluding an interest in having an adequate provision for national defense. Certainly no one in our tradition would elevate defense to an end in itself, but neither would any responsible citizen sacrifice adequate provision for defense in order to meet current consumption needs. Questions as to what constitutes an adequate allocation of resources to defense are another matter, and are not in any case questions to be decided by an economist. But there can be no contest between the national security and the claims of the consumer. We understand well enough that it is the economist's function to help show how the needs for defense can be met as efficiently as possible and with minimum disturbance to the economy as it performs its continuing function of producing goods and services for consumption.

A quite different complaint against identifying the production of goods and services for consumption as the objective of our economic system is the ancient, but every now and then repeated, protest that such an objective subordinates, if it does not destroy altogether, any interest in improving the quality of our spiritual life. What is threatened, according to this view, is the dedication to liberty and freedom, the spirit of charity, and not the least, the reflective life itself. And to some this is not just a threat but a reality in the United States.

We must reject this view not because it is entirely baseless but because it is not truly and usefully descriptive of our economic situation and because it suggests completely wrong lines of economic policy. Whatever a relative poverty of consumption goods might do for one's dedication to liberty and freedom, or to one's sense of responsibility for his fellow man, and it is not easy for me to believe that it would necessarily enhance them, I think it is true that neither our intellectual nor our artistic development is currently in danger of being corrupted by an undue affluence. No more than a small minority of academicians, at least, face any such threat. Neither does our population generally; there is ample room for the increase and improvement of consumption for the American population before we need have fears of an undue affluence. And to the extent that we face such a peril, our economy provides an easy escape. The better our economy functions in producing goods and services for consumption, the greater the scope for taking consumer satisfactions in the form of leisure. Through our history we have been able increasingly to enjoy the benefits of material prosperity in this manner. Not everyone may use leisure as you and I might most like to see it used, but this is no reason for our not pressing to the full extent of our resources to improve our efficiency in the production of consumer goods and services and in this way earn the opportunity for an expansion of leisure and, hopefully, for its beneficial use.

One more complaint on the primacy of consumption goods production should be noted. This is the protest that an excessive amount of our economic resources are devoted to the output of goods for private use and that our provision for social or public consumption is grossly inadequate. It will be recognized as the argument on "private affluence v. public squalor."

Clearly, whatever this argument has to say as to whether it is better to expand public consumption relative to private consumption, or vice versa, it has nothing whatever to say on the question of placing consumption, as such, or on the increase of consumption goods output, in first place as the objective of our economic effort. Indeed, it is totally irrelevant to this question. The only sense in which the "private affluence v. public squalor" argument might be construed as having some relevance to the question of economic objectives is if we were, by distorting the commonly accepted language of economic discourse, to regard consumption as consisting only of the use of things purchased privately and were to regard those goods and services which we obtain for final consumption through government as not being consumption at all. In this thoroughly eccentric vocabulary we would be a consumer of educational services if we went to a private school but not if we went to a public school; and we would suffer an immediate drop in the output of consumption services if, other things not changing, we were, for example, to shift the facilities for providing commuter transportation from private to public ownership.

Obviously, such a terminology would make it impossible to conduct sensible economic discourse. We can only mean by consumption goods and services those from which we seek satisfaction as final users, whether they are supplied privately or by government. Thus, the "private affluence v. public squalor" argument, while important on other grounds, is wholly irrelevant to the question whether our economic objectives may or may not be properly defined in terms of lifting the output of consumption goods and services.

There is a sense, however, in which the "private affluence v. public squalor" controversy is relevant to the question of national purpose. The relevance derives from the fact that the decisions we make on the question whether public consumption should be expanded relative to private consumption can have far-reaching effects on the institutional framework of our society. I believe that we improve and expand the opportunities which our society provides for self-directed personal development when we give every possible encouragement to private production and consumption. Similarly, I believe that we improve the position of the individual in our society and improve his opportunities for self-directed development when public production and public consumption are limited to those areas in which it is quite clear that the function involved cannot be performed at all through any practicable form of private effort or where it can be clearly demonstrated that it can be performed more efficiently through public than through private effort. This is the principle—traditional in America—that government should do for the individual what the individual cannot do at all for himself or what he cannot do as satisfactorily as government can, and that all else should be reserved for private initiative and private effort. Obviously, this philosophy of government leaves many questions as to the respective roles of public and private effort still debatable. But considering the collateral benefits that accrue in the political and noneconomic spheres of our life when we rely on private initiative rather than on centrally-directed government action, I would resolve all such doubts in favor of private initiative. This is the real question involved in the "private affluence v. public squalor" debate. It is not a question of consumption versus something else. In the end, the debate comes down to a question of how much public consumption one prefers relative to how much private consumption.

Thus, without ignoring the needs of the economy for a vigorous rate of investment in capital goods, without sacrifice of an adequate provision for national defense, without stinting in the provision of assistance to others around the world, without fear that we are corrupting ourselves in a materialist philosophy, and without prejudice to the question of private vs. public consumption, we can say that the object of our economic effort is to improve the economic well-being of our people by raising and making increasingly more efficient our capability for the production of goods and services for human consumption. But more than that we can say, also, that precisely because of the nature of our national purpose—to provide maximum opportunities for self-directed personal development—our success in this effort is greatest when we rely to the fullest possible extent on private initiative and private effort.

*   *   *   *

It is pertinent to remind ourselves that this range of issues, and in particular the question of private *vs.* public enterprise, did not escape the attention of the Congress when the Employment Act was debated and legislated in 1946. It would have been possible to write that statute so as to provide for a considerable expansion of public enterprise and for a greater degree of centralized control over private enterprise than was customary in the United States during peacetime. But the Congress quite deliberately chose not to do this. On the contrary, it chose to write the Act so as to foster and expand private competitive enterprise.

An excellent account of the evolution of the Employment Act is given in Stephen Kemp Bailey's volume, *Congress Makes a Law, The Story Behind the Employment Act of 1946.*[2] Bailey traces the development of the ideas that eventually found a place in the statute, as well as the development of some that were lost by the wayside. For present purposes, however, it will suffice to recall what the Employment Act, as it was finally enacted, has to say specifically on the institutional pattern of our economy.

In a passage that must set something of a record for length and tortuousness, even in the literature of our statute law, Section 2 of the Employment Act reads as follows:

The Congress declares that it is the continuing policy and responsibility of the Federal government to use all practicable means consistent with its needs and obligations and other essential considerations of national policy, with the assistance and cooperation of industry, agri-

2. Columbia University Press, New York, 1950.

culture, labor, and State and local government, to coordinate and utilize all its plans, functions, and resources for the purpose of creating and maintaining, *in a manner calculated to foster and promote free competitive enterprise and the general welfare,* conditions under which there will be afforded useful employment opportunities, including self-employment, for those able, willing, and seeking to work, and to promote maximum employment, production, and purchasing power.*

Thus, the Employment Act explicitly expresses the traditional preference of the American people for a reliance on private initiative and private effort in our economic life. This preference reflects, of course, a belief that enlightened self-interest parallels the public interest, which is the traditional belief of economic liberalism. It also reflects a belief, founded on experience, that an enterprise system operating through competitive markets, motivated by the prospect of private gain and guided by enlightened self-interest, is the most efficient system for meeting our economic needs.

If we have a proven wisdom on how best to organize our economy, it is that it is best organized on the basis of competitive, market-oriented and market-directed private enterprise. To be sure, we have public utilities that are organized on anything but a competitive basis, but we regulate them in a manner that is calculated to reproduce competitive results. In more than one industry, of which agriculture would be a legitimate illustration, the hand of government has reached so deeply and is so controlling that one cannot say that effective competition prevails in them. And it is a never-ending struggle to maintain competition in others. But all the same it is a market-directed competitive enterprise that is the characteristic form of our economic institu-

---

*Italics added

tions and the continuing preference of the American people. This is the basis of the Employment Act's mandate.

A significantly different approach to the problem of how best to organize our economy was actively discussed during the preparation of the Employment Act. This was the proposal for a national economic budget. As viewed by at least some of its proponents, this would have served as the foundation for full-scale national economic planning. It would have been a kind of economic blueprint that, evolving from year to year as needs and resources changed, could serve as the basis for centralized governmental allocation of economic resources in lieu of their being allocated by market forces, as in the enterprise system.

The economic problems looming up as World War II drew to a close gave more than a little encouragement to the idea that such a national economic budget was needed. There were a good many in 1946 who believed that the conversion of our economy from war to peace could never be accomplished without close governmental direction. But there was much skepticism concerning such proposals then, as there would be today.

It is instructive as well as fortunate that the task of reconversion after World War II was completed with very little direct governmental guidance, let alone control. In constant (1961) prices, federal purchases of goods and services were reduced with relatively little incident from $176 billion in 1944, of which $173 billion was for national defense, to $25 billion in 1947. And in the process the gross national product (GNP) fell only from $381 to $325 billion. It is true that unemployment rose from 670,000 in 1944 to 2,142,000 in 1947, but employment rose by around 4 million, climbing from 54 million in 1944 to 58 million in 1947. By more than anything else, the case for central planning of resource-use—the case for the national economic budget—was destroyed by the success of the predominantly market-directed reconversion that the enterprise system accomplished on its own.

Interest continues, however, in certain of the procedures suggested by the concept of a national economic budget. This interest is expressed in the suggestion that our economic performance would be improved by more systematic and extensive use of "national economic targets." It may be useful, therefore, to give some attention to these views.

It is important, first, to distinguish between forecasts and targets. Usage in these matters is rather loose and one cannot always be sure whether a figure that is put forward is meant to be a forecast or a target. But there is an important difference between the two. It is one thing to make a forecast, with or without assumptions of changes in policy, of what will be attained in a given period. It is another thing altogether to set a target which specifies quantitatively what is possible of achievement in a given period and what policy should strive to help achieve.

Making forecasts is a common undertaking and has no special interest for us in the present connection other than, perhaps, to remind us how far from their mark they may fall. The year 1962 is a good one to illustrate these failures. Early in 1962 it was officially forecast that gross national product would reach a total of $570 billion for the year as a whole. It was also forecast that the annual GNP rate in the fourth quarter of the year would reach $585 billion, in current prices. These were careful estimates of what could be expected to happen during the year and they had definite operational importance since they were the basis of official budget estimates. Actually, GNP reached only $554 billion for the year as a whole and only slightly more than $560 billion in the fourth quarter of the year (December, 1962 estimates). Thus, there was a shortfall of about $15 billion for the year as a whole and of nearly $25 billion, on an annual rate basis, during the closing months of the year.

These are large discrepancies between results as forecast and results achieved, but for our purposes more importance attaches to GNP targets than to GNP forecasts for the reason that targets have very direct and important policy implications. A forecast that fails to be borne out by the facts may have a bad effect on the economy, as the forecasting failures of 1962 doubtless had, but a GNP target, if it means what it must be interpreted as meaning, implies a definite direction of policy to be followed. The implication may not be specific as to the strategy and tactics to be pursued, but it is quite clear as to the overall direction of policy, for example, whether it should be generally expansive or restrictive.

Quantitative targets imply specific policy commitments. There are at least two potentially troublesome dangers in this. The first is that the economic context can change very quickly, indicating the need for quite a different strategy of policy. With fixed targets, widely announced, there is a danger of losing flexibility in policy. The second danger is that the policy commitment implied in a quantitative target is ill-advised and potentially very harmful if the target is an extravagant one. As targets are normally used in business and personal affairs they are deliberately set at a point that requires a certain amount of straining in order to achieve them. They may even be set quite deliberately outside the bounds of reasonable attainment. There is no a priori reason for not expecting the same overreaching in the setting of targets by government. Indeed, there is a strong presumption that specific targets as set by government will be ambitious statements of possible economic attainment, if not clearly extravagant ones. And the targets may be so inflated as to make it thoroughly unwise to direct policy to the task of achieving them.

There is a third objection to the use of targets that deserves attention. I think it is fair to say that GNP targets stated in aggregate terms, lacking any reference to the character of the output to be produced, would fail to satisfy the central economic planning enthusiasts. And I fear it is a safe forecast that the practice of setting aggregate national output targets, if continued for some time, would evolve into the practice of setting more detailed targets, and that this would approach, in its evolution, the practice of setting detailed national economic budgets. It would be only a step from setting targets for aggregate output to setting targets for the major categories of output: consumption goods, the various divisions of consumption goods, investment goods, the division of investment goods output among the various branches of industry, and so on. Ultimately, the system of allocating resources through competitive markets and of directing production by market forces would be replaced by a system of central planning and central governmental direction. Merely "indicative" planning, as it is called, is one thing, but there are potentialities inherent in it for the development of an apparatus for mandatory resource allocation completely at variance with our present economic institutions. And it would, of course, be an arrangement entirely in conflict with the requirement stated in the Employment Act, that in seeking to achieve maximum levels of employment, production and income we should use the power of government in ways that will "foster and promote free competitive enterprise."

These are some of the questions of political philosophy contained within issues which, on the surface, may seem purely economic in character. Returning to what was said at the outset concerning national purpose, that is, our desire to maintain maximum opportunity for self-directed personal development, these questions illustrate how a strategy of economic policy and its implementation can widen the scope of freedom in our society and widen opportunities for personal development, or how a policy strategy can, if unwisely designed and executed, be an obstacle to the accomplishment of our national purpose, as traditionally understood.

As indicated, the Congress did not overlook these things

when it wrote the Employment Act. The Act expresses the belief of the Congress that the institutions of a market-directed economy, in which economic power is widely diffused and continuously subject to the limits imposed by lively competition, are essential to a system of political freedom and essential to the maintenance of the open society which, for Americans, has historically been the preferred way of life and which we are determined to preserve and to strengthen in the future.

Chapter Two

Three Imperatives of Economic Policy

BEFORE TURNING TO THE QUESTIONS of economic policy to which I wish to direct attention in this second chapter, it is pertinent to emphasize again that the gravest error we can make in these important matters is to think of them as somehow not a part of, or divorced from, the social and political questions of our time, the questions that have to do with the institutional framework of our society. As I have pointed out in the preceding chapter, economic policy is never altogether neutral in these matters. Knowing this, we must shape our strategy of policy with the deliberate objective of preserving and strengthening our free institutions. We have our strictly economic objectives to achieve, to be sure, but we must strive to achieve them within an institutional framework that gives us the best chance possible to attain our paramount national purpose, which is to provide maximum opportunities to the American people for self-directed personal development.

Without a doubt, to strive to do things in this way vastly complicates the task of economic policy. The role of the economist in helping to achieve economic objectives in a market-oriented economy, no less than the roles of business management and of citizens generally, is of course a difficult one, though more to the liking of the democratic spirit. I recall an experience in one of the Iron Curtain countries in 1961 that brought this home to me rather well. My wife and I had spent the afternoon with the director of planning in the State Planning Agency of one of these countries; he was the leading economist in the state apparatus. He gave us a systematic and comprehensive account of how, as he expressed it, the "conditions of socialist production" had been established in agriculture, industry and trade. This was an entirely compulsive process, of course, and it was drenched in blood and tears, but there was no mention that afternoon of this seamy side of socialism. Our instructor for the day went on to describe in some detail the process by which his country's economic plan is developed and carried out, supplying a directive, as it does, for virtually every economic unit in the nation. When he had finished the exposition he added, in a burst of enthusiasm for his role in things, and apparently oblivious to the dreadfully drab economic performance visible to anyone looking objectively at his country's cities and villages: "You see, we have the economy in our hands."

It is not easy for me to conceive of a state of affairs more offensive to the democratic spirit. Our object is to diffuse power, including economic power, not to concentrate it. Our ideal is an economy that is in no one set of hands, but in many hands, all doing their work as nearly independently as possible. As economists, our task is to help create an environment that is favorable to independence of action and to understand the intricate workings of a market-oriented economy organized in this manner.

This is not to say that government is a passive factor in our economic life; quite the contrary. Government shoulders critically important burdens, and it is of the utmost importance that its role in this way of organizing our economic life be properly understood. It was expressed as follows in President Eisenhower's Economic Message in January, 1960:

In a free society, government makes its major contribution to economic growth by fostering conditions that encourage and reinforce the efforts of individuals and private groups to improve their circumstances. This includes the preservation and enhancement of competition, the maintenance of a stable currency, the moderation of fluctuations in employment and output, participation in the development of human and natural resources, the enhancement of personal security, provision of a sound national defense, and the maintenance of mutually advantageous ties with other countries.

This is the American system, and its hallmark is that responsibility for maintaining conditions favorable to the economy's effective operation is not carried exclusively by government, and least of all not by the federal government alone, but involves, and indeed requires, participation by state and local government, by private groups and by the citizen as an individual. The President's Message stated this as follows:

Responsibility for many of these roles is divided among the various levels of government, but none can be carried out adequately without the initiative and cooperation of individuals and private groups. This network of relationships is the product of our history. It embodies the American concept of government as the responsive instrument of the people.

We may think of this as a system of "shared responsibility," as it was repeatedly termed in President Eisenhower's Economic Reports. It is well to remind ourselves of this philosophy of government as we consider our strictly economic policy questions. Let me turn now to the major questions of economic policy as we confront them today.

*   *   *   *

The nation's strictly economic goals are stated in the Employment Act as "maximum levels of employment, production and purchasing power." Increasingly these have been merged and translated into a single goal—a higher rate of economic growth—but there has been much discussion in recent years of price stability as a second and separate goal of economic policy and to some the two have seemed to be in competition. Indeed, a belief that such an incompatibility exists between the two has led some to an outright opposition of governmental efforts to avoid inflation. But what I shall argue in this chapter is this: while there are enormously important values in price stability itself, that is, in having a monetary unit of stable purchasing power, we must understand price stability as a condition prerequisite to the attainment of vigorous and sustainable economic growth, not merely as a desirable accompaniment to it. It is not an objective of economic policy competitive with the objective of vigorous and sustainable growth; it is a condition that makes that kind of growth possible. And it derives from this essentially complementary, rather than competitive, relationship between price stability and sustainable growth that a pro-inflationist position in economic policy matters is simply untenable. An inflationist policy is simply not a viable policy. Its nonviability is notorious in an economy which, such as ours, is "open" in its international economic relationships; certainly it would be unworkable with the institutional framework we wish to preserve. To put it differently: only orthodoxy is viable in finance. We may be unorthodox without too much danger and possibly to our benefit in the style in which we have our houses built, in the music we prefer, and in dozens of other things that are important to each of us, in our fashion; but in finance we are orthodox or we are lost.

Interestingly enough, the Employment Act makes no explicit reference to price stability, either as a separate goal of economic policy or as a condition prerequisite to the achievement of an employment or growth goal. This probably reflects the fact that it was too obvious to have commanded special attention. The heavy accent which the statute places on employment, which is evident in its title and is present in different forms in several of its sections, reflects the concern felt in the closing years of World War II over the possibility that widespread unemployment would develop as a result of the conversion of economic resources from wartime to peaceful use. This was understandable in the context of the mid-forties. But it would be doing far less than justice to those who wrote and enacted the statute to say they felt no concern for stability of the price level, let alone that they were unaware of its importance as a prerequisite to the achievement of the explicit goals of the new legislation.

In any case, nowadays we think of our economic policy goals as including both the provision of maximum employment opportunities and the maintenance of a reasonable stability of prices. If it were to be written anew in today's context it would be impossible for price stability to be omitted from the Employment Act and there has even been some interest in an amendment to the statute as it stands which would make a price stability goal explicit.

The view that the goals of growth and price stability are essentially competitive rather than mutually supporting and reinforcing has, of course, enormous potentialities for producing darkness and discord in economic discourse in place of light and understanding. If one falls into the error of believing that there is a conflict between the two goals, such that one must be sacrificed for the other, it may seem that to strive for stability of prices reflects a basic deficiency in one's whole economic and social philosophy. Consider the possibilities for the demagogue: an interest in economic growth is clearly a humanistic interest; it has a direct meaning for people, through its close association with employment and jobs. Price stability, on the other hand, may be said to have little direct meaning to individuals (except money-lenders!) and little direct impact on their welfare. Thus, an interest in price stability, so the argument can go, reflects a lack of feeling for "people" and for humanistic considerations. It is not easy for such a view to be propagated in a community that has had recent experience with inflation, but it can perhaps be done in a community, such as our own, which for some generations has been spared this experience.

Furthermore, the false juxtaposition of growth and price stability produces additional overtones. The champion of "economic growth first" has no need to explain that he is an activist. A clear sense of his "activism" is carried by the word growth itself. On the other hand, an interest in price stability has a negative quality, deriving from the fact that it is, essentially, an interest in prevention; in this case in preventing inflation. A person is *for* growth, but he is *against* inflation, and in our world it is almost invariably better to be *for* than *against*. It is not easy in these circumstances to be anti-inflationist, and certainly not likely to be very popular.

But this does not mean that the advocates of "growth above all else" are necessarily explicit inflationists in matters of policy. Few of them are. The universally attractive appeal of economic growth makes it unnecessary for the advocate of "growth first," even when he does condone a degree of inflation, to make a positive case for the latter or to recommend it as a policy. True, there has been some positive argument for inflation, though very little. Most of those who have commented on the advantages of a rising price level have merely said that it helps achieve growth. In doing so they have, for the most part, merely been making observations on economic history rather than advancing proposals for deliberate economic policy. The critical point is that there is a tremendous difference between the two. Because my subject is the strategy of economic policy for the nation that is the foundation stone in the structure of Free World alliances, what I must say about the goal of a stable monetary value and about the nonviability of essentially inflationist economic and financial policies must, perforce, be very different than if my subject were not policy-oriented.

In discussions that are innocent of questions of policy, inflation is something that comes about more or less inevitably, though not intentionally, as a consequence of achieving a really satisfactory rate of economic growth. The policy-innocent inflationist regards overall price level increases as a side effect, as it were, albeit perhaps a regrettable side effect, of the process of achieving an adequate growth rate. It is only the price paid for growth, his reasoning has it, and not an excessive price, at that.

Such policy advice as this type of inflationist has to offer is typically that we should accommodate ourselves as peacefully as possible to the inevitable and certainly that we should not fight too hard to resist inflation, lest we sacrifice growth. And a battery of interesting and in some cases quite ingenious devices has been invented to help assist this peaceful accommodation. Typically, they incorporate some kind of "escalator" arrangement, such as the familiar clauses of collective bargaining agreements under which wage scales are adjusted for changes in the consumer price index. Also, arrangements have been proposed in this country, and in some cases have been adopted abroad, under which the rate of interest paid on debt instruments would be adjusted on an escalator basis, also related to changes in the level of consumer prices.

Interest in such arrangements has tended to wane of late, however, reflecting the currently more confident outlook toward the price level, and because it is becoming more and more widely recognized that escalators and related devices are at best imperfect means for achieving their intended purposes and can never be so complete or so neatly articulated to one another as to remove all inequity from the inflationary process. And there is a growing recognition that escalator devices, designed to make inflation a tolerably comfortable existence, may themselves contribute to, and accelerate, the spread of inflation. Indeed, it is seen that, carried to their logical extreme, escalators are nothing less than a formula for an instant universalizing of inflation. There is wider recognition, also, that attempts to gain an advantage in an escalated world can be carried out only by stepping up the speed of one's own escalator, or of the escalator of one's own group, and that this competitive process can end only in an inflationary chaos.

It is a fact that all the world's experience with inflation, and all the dialogue on the subject, has failed as yet to show that a broad and persisting decline in the value of money is a good thing, even when it happens inadvertently. But even if this could be shown, the showing would be irrelevant for my purposes because it would tell us absolutely nothing about what strategy of policy should be followed. The question to which we should address ourselves is not whether an upward price trend, viewed after the fact, was favorable or unfavorable to economic growth but what should be our policy, with an eye to the future, as regards price level stability.

This is a very different matter. Among other things it involves the difference between unplanned and planned inflation; between inflation that is accidental and unintended and that which is deliberate and contrived; between overall increases in prices that can be regarded as having happened in spite of policy and those for which policy must admit to some deliberate authorship.

The difference—and it is a critical difference—is between the expectational effects of inflation that are contrived, desired or even merely condoned and the expectational effects of inflation that are not only unwanted and unintended but which will not be condoned and are systematically and vigorously resisted. An inflationary psychology may develop in the second case, but it is inevitable in the first. And it is the state of individual and group psychology in these matters that is crucial.

Let us consider these expectational or psychological effects briefly. Where only a relatively slow increase of price levels has occurred, the effect is chiefly to promote an expansion of buying in excess of current requirements and normal needs as a protection against further price increases. To the extent that the inventory accumulation that this involves induces increases in economic activity and produces additional income, the process may justify itself in an expansion of sales. So far, so good, perhaps. But when inventory accumulation has outrun sales requirements by a noticeable degree, as it ultimately does, accumulation rates decline, a deflationary impact is exerted on the economy, and a danger of recession arises. The danger is all the greater, of course, if inventory accumulation is turned into depletion. And the danger that the psychology will take root in the first place is greatest, in fact is inevitable, when policy is recognized as being inflation-oriented or even merely as having an inflationary bias.

Similarly, an expectation of price increases may quicken the demand for consumer goods and businessmen may accelerate capital goods expenditures as a means of escaping the impact on their plans of expected increases in construction costs and in the prices of machinery and equipment. As in the accumulation of business inventory, there is a danger that the anticipation by consumers of their needs for goods—durable as well as nondurable—and the telescoping into the present by business concerns of fixed investment expenditure programs that might otherwise have been spread over a longer period of time, will run to excess. As this happens and as these demands finally slacken, as they ultimately will, the resulting contraction of sales must have a depressing effect on the economy.

The process may go far beyond this. Much more drastic reactions are possible if an inflationary psychology spreads and deepens, as it most certainly will if policy is deliberately inflationary. In this case, in addition to the stepped-up accumulation of business inventory and the acceleration of spending by both consumers and businesses, a speculative fever may affect financial markets, as people seek to "hedge" against inflation. But like a business inventory build-up or anticipatory buying, a speculative movement in financial markets contains within itself the seeds of its own eventual reversal. And the more widespread and rapid the movement, the greater the retreat and retrenchment that must follow in the corrective phase.

There are, of course, consequences implicit in this process and in its correction that can defeat all our efforts to achieve our economic goals. Production is set back, often very sharply; employment declines; unemployment rises; incomes are reduced. In the process, financial losses are incurred by individuals and families on a large scale and, sad to say, will be felt most severely by those least in a position to protect themselves. In the end we sacrifice economic justice as well as economic growth.

It is no escape from this conclusion to say that adequate controls can prevent this result. In a limited sense, and for a limited time, this may be true, and invariably in the world's history the result of inflation has been precisely to usher in a regime of controls. But it is precisely this that we wish to avoid. Our object is to achieve our economic goals within the framework of a free economy and not to introduce a battery of controls in its place, abandoning the institutional framework of open, competitive markets in the process. We must do it this way, however difficult, if we are to achieve our national purpose.

This means that there is no alternative to an anti-inflationary policy. Anti-inflationism is the first imperative of economic policy. No other policy will work. No other policy is viable. It is not possible for governmental policy to favor inflation. Whatever the reaction to price increases that are inadvertent, the reaction to an explicitly inflationary strategy of policy can spell nothing but disruption and a setback for the economy's growth. This is why a quite explicit and sincerely intended acceptance of reasonable price-level stability as an economic objective is an inescapable requirement of economic policy. And, as stated, it is not a goal that conflicts with the objective of high-level, sustainable economic growth but a condition prerequisite to its attainment. This is not a case in which we can take one goal and leave the other, or follow one policy and not the other. Rather, we need the one to have the other.

*   *   *   *

There has of late been a definite swing of opinion to this point of view. Indeed, I think it is not too much to say that there has been a kind of mass conversion to anti-inflationism. And the fervor of the converts, of which the federal government's Executive branch offensive in the spring of 1962 against an attempted steel price increase has certainly been the outstanding demonstration to date, is remarkable. It is not unusual, of course, for recent converts to show a zealousness in the faith from which the seasoned believer shrinks, but there were doubtless other forces also at work in the steel incident. Still, it reflects a recognition of the fact that in resisting inflation more than just a profession of faith is necessary and therein lies an important lesson for us in economic policy. Government must show, through visible evidences of policy, that it will take all reasonable steps in its power to prevent inflation. The question is how best to do this, and what is "reasonable." Let me consider this question for a moment.

There are many ways by which the federal government can show its intention to resist inflation, but of all these none is more telling than how it manages its monetary system and its budget.

But in the American governmental structure the limited degree of authority which the Executive branch, and for that matter the Legislative branch also, has over monetary policy means that special importance attaches to the federal budget. In a very real sense, the budget is the mirror of our government. It not only reflects a major part of what government does, but it is uniquely the instrument available to our Executive and Legislative authorities for implementing policy. Thus, it reflects the structure of government's policy choices.

It is true that the budget is not wholly under the control of the Executive branch, though the general shape of the fiscal plan submitted to the Congress by the President, and the theory expressed in the Budget Message which accompanies it, is a reflection of Executive branch thinking and policy intentions. Nor is the budget wholly under the control of the Legislative branch, though it is perhaps closer to this than it is to being controlled by the Executive. But the margin of control which each of these branches of our government has over the budget is a large one. And except over the short run, when existing law and administrative commitments may permit expenditures at something other than the rate which currently seems appropriate, jointly the two branches of government have complete control.

Certainly, there is enough scope for control, enough opportunity for government to show its resistance to inflation and to deploy its forces against it, that one may legitimately read policy intentions from the kind of budget that is put forward and the kind that is ultimately enacted. If there is a firm intent in government to resist inflationary tendencies, it will be evident in the budget, as will the absence of such an intent.

Thus, in a situation in which inflationary pressures are more or less continuously present, and in which they must be resisted lest an inflationary psychology be engendered, there can be no viable alternative to a budget policy that is essentially conservative. This is a second imperative of economic policy. A serious balance of payments deficit can give a special urgency to this need, as it is doing at the present time, but even in the absence of an imbalance in international payments, this second imperative of economic policy will ultimately make itself felt.

*   *   *   *

It would be a convenient and generally happy situation if conservative imperatives were encountered only in financial matters, but nowadays the problem of avoiding inflation has taken on a new dimension and conservative finance, while essential, is not enough. We need a conservative cost policy, also, and especially a conservative policy as regards labor cost. There have been periods in our history when inflationary impulses came exclusively from monetary and fiscal sources but this is no longer entirely the case. Typically, the major cause of inflation in earlier years was an excessive credit expansion, with associated money supply increases. In this context, primary emphasis could be laid on monetary and fiscal measures as ways of checking inflation and an anti-inflationary program could properly consist exclusively of credit restraint and a budgetary surplus.

This general strategy of policy and the theory of inflation which it rested on continued to command wide acceptance until 1958. At that time, however, it began to come under increasing criticism. Economic developments at the time displayed certain unique features. The economy had begun to recede slightly in mid-1957, following two years of vigorous growth, and a definite downturn occurred in the fall and winter of 1957–58. Fortunately, the decline in personal income was not very sharp, amounting to less than one percent, and total nonagricultural employment dropped by less than two percent, but elsewhere the recession left a deeper mark on the economy. The index of industrial production, in which cyclical swings are nowadays registered most heavily, fell by something over twelve percent, a sharper decline than had occurred in either 1953–54 or 1948–49, and total expenditures in GNP accounts dropped about five percent. In these circumstances one would normally not have expected price increases, but from July, 1957, the month in which the 1957–58 recession is regarded as having started, to the end of 1958 consumer prices rose by about 2.6 percent and the prices of finished manufactured goods at wholesale rose about two percent. Certainly these price increases could not be explained as resulting from a general excess of demand, nor even to have resulted from specific shortages on any significant scale. Questions were raised, accordingly, as to why the price level should be rising when aggregate demand was either not increasing at all or actually declining.

There was some tendency in this situation to explain the developments in terms of a single factor, but there were, in fact, a number of factors at work. Their range and variety was pointed out in the Economic Report of the President for January, 1959, as follows. First, there was some impact on the prices of industrial materials in 1955–56 from the side of demand. The rapid expansion of the capital goods sector of the economy in this period had certain cost- and price-increasing consequences and ultimately these spread widely through the economy. Second, there were price increases in 1957–58 in the service industries that we can interpret only as belated reactions to earlier cost increases. Third, costs were lifted in the 1955–56 experience by large-scale additions to capital and by the coming into use of new, higher cost facilities. Fourth, there was a tendency for research costs and the cost of product development to rise noticeably and for professional and technical workers to be added at considerable cost but with relatively little immediate impact on output.

But there was still another factor at work tending to induce price increases. In the mid-fifties, wages and salaries and the fringe benefits of employees rose sharply relative to productivity. As the President's Economic Report in January, 1959 pointed out, employee compensation per unit of output rose by about ten percent in the two-year period 1956–57, after having been roughly constant between 1953 and 1955. This was the new factor in inflation: a rise in unit costs of production, as money wage rates and fringe benefit expenses rose faster than the improvements that could be achieved in productivity. It had an impact on the prices of many final products and services but where, for one reason or another, cost increases could not be passed on to the buyer in higher prices it compressed profit margins. Thus it had a twin effect: tending to raise prices; and, by suppressing profit, tending to stifle economic growth.

There was considerable resistance to the view that increases in labor cost per unit of output were a factor in the 1957–58 price level rise. There was equal resistance to the thought that they could be an adverse factor in achieving our growth objectives. A sampling of this resistance is reflected in the hearings before the Joint Economic Committee in January, 1959. The Council of Economic Advisers found itself in the center of the debate and in an effort to present a balanced view of the cost and price history of the period which would register the labor-cost effect but not overdo this factor, I wrote as follows to one member of the Congress in February, 1959, in response to a written inquiry:

In my judgement, increases in wages and other employee compensation have been a major factor making for the price increases that have occurred since mid-1956, and these price increases have in turn been a major factor in limiting real demand. But wage increases were not the only factor at work. The rapid expansion of capital in recent years, reaching boom proportions in 1956, added materially to the cost and price rise; and I would not entirely absolve government from responsibility for some part of the end result. To a large extent the momentum of the rise was due to the expectation that costs and prices would be still higher later on and so-called escalator clauses assured the rapid spread of increases through the economy.

As time has passed, the role of rising unit costs as a factor tending to inflate prices and to suppress economic growth has been more widely recognized. Indeed, by 1962 means for somehow limiting increases in labor costs to productivity improvements had been made a major element in federal economic policy, and properly so. The difficulty of stabilizing unit costs without interfering unduly in the collective bargaining process has been widely acknowledged too, and I fear it must be recognized that there is much skepticism nowadays as to chances of accomplishing it. Thus, a new problem in the strategy of economic policy has been created. It may be stated briefly as follows: if the means available to government for preventing money costs of production from outstripping improvements in productivity are unequal to the task, federal economic policy may be compelled, in an effort to preserve price level stability and to assure sustainable growth, to employ a mix, as it were, of monetary and fiscal policy that will impose dangerously heavy restraints on the economy.

Let us consider the consequences for the economy of heavy and continuing use of monetary and fiscal measures for containing a push on prices originating from the side of costs. It will suffice to call attention to three specific consequences, though there are more.

First, a restrictive monetary policy, and a supporting debt-management policy, that is, a policy aimed at doing as much federal financing and refinancing as possible out of current savings, has a tendency to produce levels of interest rates, especially of long-term interest rates, appreciably higher than would otherwise prevail and potentially restrictive of the economy's growth. Investment-type expenditures of business, and to some extent consumer expenditures, too, feel the restraint, as is intended, but the impact on the economy is uneven. It tends to bear more heavily on small business than on large business; it is especially repressive of capital improvement programs to be undertaken by individuals and institutions of limited means, notably the typical prospective home buyer, because he normally finds it necessary to borrow on a long-term basis. Thus, among the effects of heavy and continuing reliance on restrictive monetary policy are a more or less continuing repression of smaller units in the business community, a restraint on home building and home buying, and a dampening of business investment incentives where long-term debt financing is required.

The second of the consequences is that a restrictive monetary and credit policy favors the extension of public enterprise, and of the federal government's activities in particular. This comes about in several ways. First, high and rising long-term interest rates usually act as a damper on the public improvement programs of state and local governments that have to compete for funds in the open market but, apart from debt-service costs, they have little or no effect on the expenditures of the federal government, whether for capital improvement programs or for current operating functions. Second, when interest rates are high, the pressure for the federal government to supply loan funds at interest rates below the market is enormous, and the Congress, in recent years, has shown a willingness to accede liberally to it. The result is a vast expansion of federal credit-extending activities. And high costs of borrowing by local authorities become a reason for seeking direct federal aid, as for education, road building, urban redevelopment, the construction of hospital and related facilities, etc.

The third important consequence of extended and heavy use of restrictive monetary and fiscal policies to prevent price inflation where cost inflation is the actual cause, or a major element in it, is on the profit margins of business concerns and thus on investment and growth. Where monetary restraint manages, in alliance with such other conditions as a significant margin of unused domestic capacity and increasingly sharp foreign competition to prevent prices from increasing, profit margins are narrowed and economic growth is retarded. This, sad to say, is a fair, brief summary of much of the history of the past few years.

To date, efforts to break out of this policy dilemma have been limited to appeals for voluntary restraints on cost increases, notably on wage increases, that exceed productivity improvements and on unwarranted price advances. The appeal was put as follows in the January, 1957 Economic Report:

Economic developments in recent years show the basic role that monetary and fiscal restraints must play if the excesses that often accompany prosperity are to be avoided. At the same time, this experience suggests that fiscal and monetary policies must be supported by appropriate private policies to assure both a high level of economic activity and a stable dollar. When production, sales and employment are high, wage and price increases in important industries create upward pressures on costs and prices generally. To depend exclusively on monetary and fiscal restraints as a means of containing the upward movement of prices would raise serious obstacles to the maintenance of economic growth and stability. In the face of a continuous upward pressure on costs and prices, moderate restraints would not be sufficient; yet stronger restraints would bear with undue severity on sectors of the economy having little if any responsibility for the movement toward a higher cost-price level and would court the risk of being excessively restrictive for the economy generally (p. 44).

And further in the same report:

The full burden of avoiding price inflation, which is an ever present hazard in an expanding economy operating close to capacity, cannot be successfully carried by fiscal and monetary restraints alone. To place this burden on them would invite the risk of producing effects on the structure and functioning of our economy which might, in the years ahead, impair the vitality of competitive enterprise. And failure to accept the responsibilities inherent in a free economy could lead to demands that they be assumed by government, with the increasing intervention and loss of freedom that such an approach inevitably entails. The successful extension of prosperity with price stability must be a cooperative effort in which the policies of individuals and economic groups and of all levels of Government are consistent with one another and mutually reinforcing (p. 3).

President Kennedy's initiative in January, 1962 to set forth guidelines for wage increases that would be consistent with the achievement of adequate growth was a constructive additional move aimed at meeting this problem. It has been far from fully successful to date, but it has been helpful on balance, in my judgment. I will return to the wage guidelines with some suggestions for their further development.

At the level of strategy, this is the major policy problem confronting us today: how to restrain cost increases and prevent price inflation without recourse to monetary and fiscal measures that will, in the end, retard economic growth to rates significantly below those attainable. In this we find the third imperative of economic policy: the need to preserve a reasonable overall stability of unit labor cost.

A proper understanding of these matters provides a basis for understanding, in turn, why our economy in recent years has tended to experience a rate of growth that is below what may be reasonably regarded as its potential. And it provides a basis for understanding also why we have witnessed some acceleration in recent years in the substitution of public for private enterprise, especially in financial areas. Although we have no basis for being sanguine as to the prospect for finding an entirely agreeable solution to these difficult problems, to recognize their character is, of course, a major step toward finding a solution to them.

As the 1957 Economic Report suggested, it may well be that the approach we take to this complex of problems will govern not only our success in achieving a satisfactory rate of economic growth, but will govern also our success in preserving and strengthening the institutions of privately-owned, market-directed competitive enterprise as the framework within which to conduct our economic activity. It will, accordingly, have much to do with the success we have in achieving our national purpose.

Chapter Three

Some Recent Lessons of Experience on the Use of Economic Policy Measures

---

ALTHOUGH WE MUST ADMIT to a tendency to exaggerate the problems of our own times, it does seem that the present context is an unusually difficult one for which to design an appropriate strategy of economic policy. Formidable obstacles appear in the path of all acceptable policy approaches.

First, in the present context, with a large and continuing deficit in the balance of international payments and with a very large volume of foreign-held liquid claims outstanding against the United States dollar, there is little scope for the use of monetary ease as a means of promoting a higher rate of growth. Indeed, the pro-inflationist approach to the growth problem has been thoroughly discredited. There is much wider appreciation today than formerly that much more is involved in the relation of our costs and prices to those in other advanced industrial nations than merely our position in world trade. What is involved is the financial strength and posture of the leading reserve-currency country of the world and, even more than that, the strength and viability of the far-ranging alliances that underlie the Free World system. And these are things not to be put needlessly at risk. What this has meant in the practical language of economic strategy is that the case for easy money as a solution to the problem of inducing a higher pitch of economic activity at home has been totally destroyed. And it is not likely to be revived soon. There appears to have been some small improvement in 1962 in our international payments deficit, but the problem remains serious. Certainly there is no present prospect that we can ignore it in shaping economic policy. A return to inflationism, accordingly, or even to moderately easy money as a solution to the growth problem cannot be looked for in the calculable future.

Furthermore, the continuing need to resist cost-induced inflation and the unavailability of means for doing this directly except through a combination of moral suasion, the pronouncement of wage guidelines, and occasional sallies by government into collective bargaining situations—inadequate to the task even in concert—more or less compels recourse to a generally restrictive monetary policy, even though this tends to retard the economy's growth.

Yet the need for a generally expansionist strategy of policy is widely recognized. Indeed, it is perhaps more obvious now than ever before that the problem of how best to improve our economic performance is a persistent one, not likely to be dissolved in a standard business cycle expansion. If it wasn't obvious before, this became quite clear in 1962. Contrary to official forecasts, and to some private expectations, the economy staged only a barely adequate recovery from the mild and short-lived recession of 1960–61. Employment lagged noticeably, especially in the goods-producing sector of our economy. The unemployment ratio in the fall of 1962 was still only slightly below six percent, despite a distinct slowing down in the rate of increase of the civilian labor force. And to lend a dimension of familiarity to the situation, the cost of living was continuing to rise at something over one percent a year. Once again we were confronted with the combination of a slow growth rate, relatively high unemployment, less than full utilization of industrial capacity, and increases in the cost of living.

It is not surprising that in this atmosphere of disappointing recovery and virtually all-round policy frustration an active search has been made for new approaches to the task of stimulating the economy while maintaining reasonably stable prices. And it is not surprising that, easy money having been incapacitated, so to speak, as a policy approach, interest has heightened in the possibility of spurring the economy by means of an easy fiscal policy. I should like, therefore, to examine certain of the fiscal approaches to the task of stimulating our economy that nowadays command particular favor.

*   *   *   *

Because budgetary deficits are so prominent in these policy approaches or strategies, interest has heightened of late in questions of budget presentation. Let me comment briefly, first, on this problem; we can then turn to the merits of specific fiscal policy measures, notably to increases in the levels of federal spending and to tax reduction.

Without pursuing matters of budget presentation to an uncalled-for extent, it may be noted briefly that the consolidated cash budget or statement, as it is commonly called, is to be preferred over the administrative budget both because it provides information in a form that fits better the categories of economic analysis and because it gives a more comprehensive view of federal financial transactions. This does not, however, diminish the importance of the administrative budget. This conventional budget statement is essential for the conduct of our governmental system and, for this reason if for no other, must be respected.

Nowadays a third type of statement, the national-income accounts statement of federal financial transactions—the federal sector of the national-income accounts—is attracting a good deal of attention and deserves special comment. First, although it is more prominent nowadays than formerly, the national-income accounts statement is not new. A reconciliation of the national-income accounts statement with the conventional administrative budget and with the consolidated cash statement for the years 1958 through 1960 will be found, for example, in President Eisenhower's Economic Report for January, 1961 and similar materials will be found in earlier reports. In the January, 1956 Report, for example, federal financial statements in the form of national-income accounts are given for the years 1950 through 1955.

Second, the special utility of the federal sector of the national-income accounts in the analysis of the impact of federal financial transactions on the economy is most often attributed to the fact that these accounts are compiled on an accrual rather than on a cash or current basis. That is, corporate profits taxes are included in federal receipts not when they are paid to the Treasury but when the liability for their eventual payment originates. Similarly, federal expenditures for goods enter the national-income accounts as of the time the goods are delivered, not when payments for them are actually made. And so on.

This style of accounting has certain advantages for revealing the impact of the fiscal operations of government on the economy, but it has certain disadvantages, too. The accrual of tax liabilities, for example, is a significant incident for a business concern, but so also is the actual out-payment of cash to cover liabilities accrued at an earlier date. For some purposes it is important to know when the liabilities were incurred; for other purposes it is important to know when the liabilities were discharged.

Also, the national-income accounts are less comprehensive than the consolidated cash statement in that they exclude capital and lending transactions. This is a particularly significant omission in view of the volume of these transactions. It is estimated, for example, that disbursements under major federal credit programs in the fiscal year 1963 will amount to something over $8 billion and that repayments will come close to $6 billion. Obviously, we cannot ignore these transactions if we are to have a complete account of how federal finances are affecting the economy.

The national-income accounts statement has a unique value, perhaps, in that its timing of transactions may serve best to test the question whether our tax system puts a brake on economic expansion at an early stage in a cyclical recovery. Actually, it suggests that this is the case, but whether there is in fact a braking effect can be known only when capital and lending operations have been incorporated into the statement. It would be essential also to a test of this alleged braking effect to determine whether the accrual of tax liabilities has the same effect on business operations as the actual payment of taxes, and whether the impulses sent into the economy at the date of delivery of goods to the federal sector are different and more significant to business enterprise than the impulses sent out by the government's actual payment of cash and its receipt by the supplier. These would be very fruitful areas for research.

Finally, it should be borne in mind that both the administrative budget and the consolidated cash statement data are available more promptly than national-income accounts data. As of this writing (November 2, 1962), for example, administrative budget data and seasonally adjusted data on federal cash receipts and payments are available through September, 1962, but the most recent publicly available data on the federal income and product account do not extend beyond June 30. The quality of being up-to-date is not to be underestimated in economic statistics, especially if they are to be used in policy formulation. By this criterion, national-income accounts for the federal sector are as yet far less than fully satisfactory.

There are also occasional expressions of interest in the so-called capital budget, an older style of presentation which, though not used by our federal government, is employed in various forms in other countries. Its chief feature is that it separates current-type expenditure transactions, those that are to pay, e.g., for services and for nondurable goods, from capital-type transactions, e.g., for a public building with a long service life and continuing value as an asset. The thought is that a deficit incurred on current account should be distinguished from one incurred on capital account. Perhaps so, but a budget statement that would make this distinction—and you will find on reflection that the distinction can be made only very arbitrarily in many cases—would indicate no particular handling of the cash-v.-accrual question of accounting, would have no special claim to comprehensiveness, and would have no special merit for revealing the impact of federal expenditures on the economy.

The moral of all of this is that while no one of these styles of budget presentation is perfect, we can make good use of all of them provided, of course, that budget accounting systems do not proliferate to the point where the citizen will be helpless to follow what is going on in his country's finances. What irony it would be for a democratic country if a richness of budget information should serve to obscure rather than clarify.

*   *   *   *

For our purposes, the significant point is that a lag in the economy has persisted in the face of budgetary deficits, however calculated. Let me turn, therefore, to the measures of fiscal policy—expenditure acceleration and emergency tax reduction—now so frequently proposed as means for stimulating the economy.

I believe there are some lessons that can be learned from re-

cent history as to the effectiveness of government expenditure increases as a means of promoting a higher rate of growth. Certainly it must be conceded that 1962's economic lag cannot be
attributed to any failure of federal spending to rise. On the contrary, in the conventional administrative budget, net budget expenditures in fiscal 1962 were $6.2 billion higher than in fiscal
1961. And federal expenditures in fiscal 1961 were another $5
billion higher than in fiscal 1960. Thus, in a two-year span, net
budget expenditures have increased $11.2 billion, about equally
divided between expenditures for defense and for other purposes.
No one will ever know what might have been the result had we
been able, between fiscal 1960 and fiscal 1962, to cut taxes by
$11.2 billion instead of having had an $11.2 billion increase in
net budget expenditures, but what we had was the latter and yet
the economy has been far from spirited. I think we may conclude
from this experience that if the atmosphere is not favorable to an
expansion of private spending, an increase in federal expenditures, even a large and rapidly accelerating increase, will not necessarily produce an appreciable and continuing rise in overall
economic activity.

Yet we must not ignore the short-term impact on the economy that can be produced by federal expenditure acceleration. I
think there must have been considerable acceleration of spending in the second half of 1962 and in a limited sense the exercise
seems to have accomplished its purpose. In any case, a rather
sharp rise in federal spending levels, mainly in the defense and
space programs, coincided in mid-1962 with a slowdown in the
private sector of the economy. As I have indicated, the result
seems to be that recession has been deferred but the economy
still lacks outstanding strength and the momentum of recovery is far from permanently assured. And so far as producing
long-term growth is concerned, the evidence of the experiment,
if it may be termed that, suggests total failure. Worse than that,

spending has been elevated to a level so far out of line with tax receipts that the prospects of bringing the two into balance has been rendered quite dim.

There are a priori grounds, too, for skepticism as to the effectiveness of expenditure acceleration as a countercyclical measure. In the first place, it must be borne in mind that in an economy such as ours, in which periods of contraction have of late been of relatively short duration, expenditure adjustments must be carried through on a very fast schedule if they are to be helpful in recession and early recovery and if a belated increase in expenditures is to be prevented from complicating the expansion phase of the cycle. Extensive preliminary planning and a continual state of readiness are necessary if useful results are to be produced. But the fact is that there are severe limitations on the number of projects the scheduling of which can be usefully adjusted for this purpose.

Perhaps I may be permitted to illustrate the type of problem involved in this connection by a personal anecdote. When efforts were being made early in 1957 to marshal resources at the government's disposal to help prevent the onset of economic contraction and to moderate any downturn that might occur, a project was noted that was well-fitted to one of the constraints under which the program was of necessity being conducted. Because the federal debt at the time was close to its legal maximum, and because it was impossible as a practical matter to obtain an adjustment of the ceiling from the Congress, a distinct advantage inhered in any project that could be carried through outside the confines of the administrative budget. Such a project was discovered. It was a much needed building for a federal agency which was in a position to meet the construction costs out of trust-fund accumulations. The necessary encouragement was promptly given to its initiation, though no one with an understanding of the time schedules involved in these things expected any help, except after considerable delay, from the construction activity that would result. But I doubt that it would have occurred to anyone that the lag between the initiation of the project and the actual undertaking of construction would have spanned two full business cycles. All the same, the fact is that work on this structure began only in time to be useful, countercyclically, in the summer of 1962.

I would like to believe that this is not a typical case, but I am troubled by the thought that it may be. It is typical at least of cases where no preliminary planning, site selection, ground acquisition, etc., has been completed. I believe it illustrates fairly the proposition that, while we may make some contribution to the short-run stabilization of our economy by the acceleration of expenditures on already planned and funded projects, there is little if anything to be gained, so long as the business cycle continues to be of relatively short duration, from undertakings not already well-advanced in these respects.

Also, it must be borne in mind that the natural history of federal expenditure programs is that they increase continuously, not that they fluctuate up and down in some reasonable relation to the short-term business cycle. Accordingly, when such programs are undertaken we must be quite sure of our ability to carry the higher level of expenditures permanently. Specific programs may fluctuate, but the aggregates, which are what determine fiscal burden, have tended to rise almost continuously. For example, federal budget expenditures for natural resource development have increased since 1946 in every fiscal year but three. What this means is that, while expenditure acceleration may give some upward thrust to the economy in the short term, it can have a more or less lasting impact on the budget. Thus, we must judge the wisdom of entering expenditure acceleration programs with an eye to our ability to carry the new level of spending permanently.

Summarizing, the lessons of experience are that relatively little timely countercyclical benefit can be obtained from federal expenditure acceleration, and that it offers no real hope of producing a durably high level of economic growth. Clearly, we will be well-advised to place major emphasis on the development of an expenditure program that will make genuine contributions to the improvement and rounding-out of our economic base and to our capability for economic growth and, because it is so sized as to be well within the limits of what can be financed from tax receipts over the cycle, can be sustained over a long period.

*   *   *   *

Let me turn now to a second approach to the task of helping to stabilize our economy, namely, emergency-type tax reduction. There are few questions in the areas of public policy that have been more extensively discussed in recent years. The issue was actively debated in 1957–58; it was the subject of an almost equally spirited discussion in 1960–61; and we had a third such exercise in the summer of 1962.

Still the subject is surrounded by questions. No one can say with certainty, even in a specific cyclical situation let alone as a general proposition, whether a temporary reduction of taxes to head off a threatened recession or to reverse a recession already under way will produce a significant increase in production and employment. That it will itself contribute to an increase in after-tax income is obvious, but whether its contribution will more than offset such income-reducing forces as may also be at work and how it might compare in this respect with other possible moves cannot be foretold with any assurance. And the extent to which such direct income effect as is registered will produce in increase in consumption expenditures and in production and employment is far from certain.

It may have seemed in the summer of 1962 and later in the

year that there was a wide consensus on the economic impact of tax reduction, but this was not the case. In the first place, there were wide disparities in the proposals then being made. Some favored tax cuts that would be temporary. Others called for permanent reductions. Some suggested reductions designed to increase after-tax income for all personal taxpayers, hoping thereby to give a significant boost to consumption expenditures and thence to employment and income. Others proposed reductions primarily to reduce the burden of taxes on business concerns, in the hope that employment and income would be increased by lifting business investment expenditures. In the second place, some advocates of tax-cutting argued strongly that the reductions should be accompanied by equivalent or near-equivalent reductions in federal spending while others regarded concurrent reductions in federal spending as certain to negate any beneficial effects from a tax change. Thus, beneath the apparent consensus were numerous and fundamental disagreements.

We must somehow find a way through this tangle. Let us begin by considering the merits of a temporary cut in the rates levied against the lower brackets of personal income, designed to bolster consumer demand and unmatched by any expenditure reduction.

No one can be quite sure how other individuals, or even large groups of individuals, will react to such a change in their tax status, but it would seem reasonable to expect that a tax cut planned to be temporary and so understood by the taxpayers would have a less stimulative effect in the economy than a tax reduction that is confidently expected to be permanent. But the reaction would doubtless vary with the amount of the reduction. If the increase in after-tax income is very small it may well be lost in the family budget and, being hardly noticeable, would probably be spent in full as received. On the other hand, a temporary cut of substantial size, from the taxpayer's point of view, would probably be saved to a greater extent and thus cushioned in its impact on consumer demand. The reactions might be the opposite, however. A large reduction might be an invitation to dissaving through the incurrence of debt and a small reduction might increase savings by being used to pay an overdue bill.

There are cushioning effects also in the relation between such increases in consumption expenditures as are induced by tax reduction and the increases that might be induced in the volume of production and employment. Production increases would be frustrated altogether, or held to amounts less than proportionate to the increase in consumer spending, if increases in sales are met out of inventories. Further, to the extent that an inventory reduction, induced by a higher volume of sales, leads to a reduction in business debt to the banking system, the multiplier effect is still further lessened. And even if current production schedules are increased, generating a further increase in incomes, this would doubtless involve a less than proportionate increase in employment, since the needed adjustment might be made by increasing the average number of hours worked per week.

Other cushioning effects could be described, but these will suffice to show that there are ample grounds for having reservations concerning the expansive effect of temporary tax reduction. And needless to say, the chances that these cushioning effects will make themselves felt is greater when there is uneasiness about the economic outlook than when the economy is clearly on the mend or when an upward momentum has been strongly established. If emergency tax reduction measures are undertaken during a recession, when psychology is at its worst, the cushioning of their impact, unfortunately, is likely to be considerable. Cushioning might be less in the early phases of a recession, or on its eve, but in recent years recessions have not been recognizable as such until after they have been under way for a few months. And normally the case for tax reduction is not easy to make until recession is rather obvious.

And thought must also be given to the budgetary impact of tax reduction. Indeed, revenue-loss considerations are likely to be decisive in the end, and these are such that tax reductions, even temporary ones, that are of really significant size from the point of view of the taxpayer may well be ruled out. Because we have more than fifty million taxpayers, a tax reduction which would add $2.50 a week, on the average, to the family budget—not, after all, a large income change—would involve a revenue loss of something in the neighborhood of $5 billion a year. And although it would reduce individual income tax collections by about 10 percent, it would raise personal consumption expenditures by something less than 1.5 percent, as a direct impact, and possibly by no more than 3 percent considering its secondary and subsequent effects. Obviously, a tax reduction that would have a really large impact on consumption expenditures would involve a staggering loss of revenues for the federal budget.

Finally, there is a time dimension of this budgetary effect that must be considered. While a tax reduction undertaken as a temporary measure may prove to be less effective than a permanent cut, the irony of it is that a cut intended to be temporary may in fact prove to be permanent. Tax changes are of necessity made in a political context; indeed, they are normally handled in a context that is highly charged politically and it is a fair general observation that it is far easier, as a political matter, to reduce taxes than it is to increase them. Supporting this rudimentary political maxim I should like to put to you a question that is hypothetical in the extreme but is nonetheless instructive, to wit: could you identify a point in the history of the last ten years when it might have been desirable to have increased taxes as a means of dampening a boom that might have followed any tax reduction of the type and dimensions that might, as a practical matter, have been enacted? No one can be sure, of course, of his answer to a question as hypothetical as this, but it is impossible for this witness to conceive of a situation in recent years when the indicated circumstances would have prevailed. In offering a temporary tax cut we would lose the psychological advantage that inheres in offering something that can be regarded as lasting, but if the tax cut's stimulative impact were insufficient, as it might well be, the chances of terminating it would be negligible and we would be left with no lasting stimulus to the economy and an eroded tax-gathering capability.

From this I conclude that, as a strategical matter, it is best to strive for tax reduction that can be permanent and which will enhance the economy's underlying vigor and which is so sized that because it can be afforded in the fiscal sense over a reasonable period of time, will leave the fiscal position of the federal government strengthened rather than impaired.

Finally, what of the impact on the economy of the budgetary deficits in which expenditure increases and tax reductions are likely to be reflected in the short run and possibly also in the long run? I would not want to argue that recent history has been absolutely clear and complete in what it has to tell us about the effect of budgetary deficits on the economy. But there are some interesting and instructive lessons in it for us.

Notably, there is the fact that we have had a string of deficits without signs of their having started any unusual momentum in the economy or even of their having been favorable to the spread of such impulses as have been generated from other sources. We had a deficit in the fiscal year 1962 in the conventional or so-called administrative budget of $6.3 billion, and this followed a deficit of close to $4 billion in the previous fiscal period. No official estimate of the budgetary outcome for fiscal

1963 has been published as of this date, but it seems likely that something between $6 and $8 billion may be expected.[1] Similarly, the deficit in the federal government's consolidated cash statement increased from $2.3 billion in fiscal 1961 to $5.7 billion in fiscal 1962 and will doubtless persist in fiscal 1963, if current indications of the outcome in the administrative budget are borne out by events. Finally, federal income and product accounts have shown deficits for seven consecutive quarters, through the second quarter of the calendar year 1962, the last period for which these data are at present available (October-November, 1962).

True, these are not contrived deficits in the sense that they have been brought about by tax reductions, but neither are they merely reflections of a recession in tax receipts. Actually, net budget receipts were higher in fiscal 1962 than in fiscal 1961, and higher in the first three months of fiscal 1963 than in the comparable three months of fiscal 1962. Considered through the third quarter of 1962, cash receipts from the public have likewise been increasing. There is, therefore, a strong element of contrivance in the deficits and they must be evaluated in these terms.

As such, the experience should give us pause. It suggests no curative effect in deficits, as such; what is more, it suggests the possibility that we are developing a chronic budgetary deficit, persisting even at what could well be the top of a cycle. It is not unusual for the federal budget to show a larger deficit in the fiscal year that follows the one in which the trough of a recession occurs. In the 1958–59 recovery, for example, the federal deficit was substantially larger in fiscal 1959 than in fiscal 1958. But in the present situation we have a large deficit in the second full fiscal year following the recession trough, and it is larger than

---

1. An official (Bureau of the Budget) estimate of $7.8 billion was made in November, 1962, but less than two months later this was raised to $8.8 billion.

the deficit in the first full post-trough fiscal period. To make matters worse, a still larger deficit seems to be in store for the third full fiscal year following the recession trough. We had better pull ourselves out of this situation because latent in chronic budgetary deficits there is, of course, the threat of full-scale, old-fashioned monetary inflation.

*   *   *   *

Let me add a word on what is, in a sense, the major strategical aspect of these questions, namely, the harmonization of fiscal policy tactics with the moves followed in other areas, notably in monetary policy.

Harmonization of policy is an absolute requirement. To try, for example, to stimulate through a step-up of federal spending an economy that is being retarded by a restrictive money policy would be worse than merely futile: in addition to having little net expansive effect on the economy such a mixture of policy would increase the scope of government at the expense of the private sector of the economy and ultimately reshape the institutional structure of our economy, without public consent in any meaningful sense, in the direction of some species of statism.

Similarly, it would be a largely futile and even dangerous undertaking to try to stimulate by tax reduction an economy that was being restrained by monetary policy. Nothing could be gained from a policy tug-of-war of this kind; in the process the revenue-raising capability of the government, and its capability for satisfactorily performing the essential functions of government would be dangerously eroded.

A policy mix of this latter type has been suggested by the OECD as appropriate for the United States at this time, considering our balance of payments deficit. But the possibility that the position of the dollar might be less disturbed by an easy fiscal policy aimed at spurring the domestic economy than by an easy money policy designed to serve the same purpose does not at all suggest that a policy mix involving large federal deficits and relatively high interest rates would necessarily be expansive on balance. What is clearly indicated as needed in such a situation is a durable correction of the balance of payments deficit which will permit the several arms of policy to be used in harmony rather than at cross purposes. Lacking this, the continued erosion of the tax base, without an adequate associated expansion in the economy, may cause a serious impairment of the government's revenue-gathering capability.

There is a time dimension, also, in the harmonization of stabilization policy. Clearly, it would be a needless and unwise exercise to undertake emergency tax reduction when a move to induce a higher level of activity is already under way from the side of monetary policy and, in the circumstances, can reasonably be expected to have some success. Forebearance is required here, though this is not a popular stand when there are strong demands for tax reduction.

Certainly, recent experience teaches the need for forebearance in having recourse to expenditure acceleration and tax reduction as elements in an anti-recession strategy. A number of considerations suggested the need for caution in 1957–58. In this case there were certain changes in the tax laws to be obtained, and in order not to complicate these legislative issues by simultaneous consideration of an emergency tax cut the latter was deferred in order first to dispose of the former. In the end, the economy turned into a recovery phase before an appropriate occasion for tax reduction arose. Looking back on the incident, some have speculated that the recovery would have been more vigorous and of longer duration had the tax cuts been made. Perhaps so, but no one could have said so at the time. Nor can anyone say so now, for that matter, except as sheer speculation. And illustrating the need for harmonization of policy, if tax cuts in 1958 would have been an occasion for an even more restrictive credit policy than did in fact prevail in 1959 in the absence of tax reduction, the exchange would have been a poor one, indeed.

Events in the year 1962 were also instructive. Who can say that if taxes had been cut in the summer of 1962 the trend of activity during the remainder of the year and in 1963 would have been more to our standard of optimum performance? When the 1962 decision not to reduce taxes was taken the economy was lagging, but it was not declining. There were ample grounds for the view that what was needed was not a temporary cut in taxes to help prevent a recession that no one could be sure was actually coming and which as things turned out did not come, but a basic restructuring of the tax system designed to promote a higher level of long-term growth. No one can be entirely sure, but the chances are that to have cut taxes in the summer of 1962 to the extent and in the manner that they most likely would have been cut, had they been cut, would have had little effect on the course of the economy, would have had no effect whatever on the level of federal spending, but would have prejudiced the chances of undertaking in 1963 the first installment of a program of incentive-increasing, growth-promoting tax reduction and reform. This, too, would have been a very bad bargain.

Looking back over the history of recent years, and having in mind the currently popular view that an easy fiscal policy is appropriate in a situation in which an easy money policy is not practical, relevant lessons in economic strategy are found. The first is that the opportunities for helping to stabilize activity through the acceleration of public construction or procurement programs under way or at least well-advanced are rather severely limited, and that what we need rather than an off-again, on-again program designed and administered with the hope of eliminating cyclical fluctuations is a carefully planned, long-term program of public construction designed to improve our basic productive capacity and our welfare and well within the fiscal capability of the government.

Second, in the area of tax reduction, evidence against the wisdom of temporary tax-cutting measures is increasing. It becomes steadily clearer that what is called for is a permanent restructuring of our tax system, designed with long-range benefits in mind. And to the extent that this involves tax reduction, as it should, the amount of the revenue loss must be manageable within the context of a budget that can be brought to balance at reasonably high levels of economic activity.

Finally, what we know from experience as to the need for policies that work together rather than at cross-purposes suggests that the greatest need in the present situation is for an elimination of the balance of payments deficit, which would make it possible for monetary and fiscal policy to join forces. Lacking a correction of the payments deficit, fiscal ease, without having the desired expansive effect on the economy, may have the result mainly of expanding the scope of government relative to the private sector of the economy and undermining the tax-gathering capability of government. Obviously, we must have a strategy of policy that will avoid these results.

Chapter Four

Essentials of a Strategy of Economic Policy

I CHOSE TO BEGIN this volume with a discussion of national purpose because a strategy of economic policy, if it is to be worthy of that name, must be guided by a concept of the kind of world in which we want to live and designed quite specifically to help achieve it. Our strategy should, of course, help improve our economic performance, but it should do this in a manner that will enhance the opportunities which our social and economic system affords for self-directed personal development and fulfillment. As the Employment Act suggests, we must strive to achieve our economic objectives—high and rising levels of production, employment and purchasing power—in a manner that will "foster and promote free competitive enterprise."

There is a parallel requirement as regards the impact of economic policy on the structure and operations of government. Our concept of national purpose implies a preference for limited government. It implies a preference for the kind of government

57

that is closest to the individual and in which the individual has maximum practical opportunity personally to participate. The strategy of policy that will serve us best, accordingly, is a strategy that gives encouragement to the development of local and state government and avoids a transfer of its functions increasingly to the more distant, less accessible federal government.

Because the economic policy choices we make can carry us farther from a system of competitive enterprise and can cause the role of local and state government to be lessened as the federal establishment is expanded, we must ask the following questions of any economic strategy. Will it enlarge the scope of individual liberty or will it reduce it? Will it provide greater incentives to individual initiative and effort and to private enterprise or will it weaken these incentives and encourage greater reliance on government? Will it weaken local and state government and promote, in their stead, an extension of government at the federal level?

These are primarily political questions, to be sure, but in the end, and in the larger dimensions of policy to which we must be alert in a democracy, it is precisely in such political questions that we find the important differences between one design of economic strategy, one approach to our economic objectives, and another.

*   *   *   *

Turning now to the more strictly economic aspects of our problem, let us consider the policies that will serve best, at this time, to improve the performance of our economy. Clearly, the need is for an expansionist policy. This has been perfectly clear since early in 1962, when it became apparent that the recovery from the mild and short-lived 1960–61 recession was to be a disappointment, and it has continued to be perfectly clear to this date. What is more, the need for an expansionist policy is almost certain to continue well into the decade. If this proves not to be the case, strategy can be adjusted as needed, but at the moment the need for an expansionist policy seems likely to be a durable one. The question is how best to provide the needed stimulus.

On this question there are two principal points of view. There is first the theory that the shortfall of production in recent years below what may reasonably be regarded as the economy's potential output has been due to an inadequacy of consumption demand. This leads to the suggestion that a direct increase in consumption demand—provided either by an immediate across-the-board individual income tax reduction, by a faster rate of increase in money wage rates, or by stepped-up federal expenditures, or by some combination of these—is needed to quicken the tempo of private sector activity. Some indirect impact on investment goods demand is looked for from such a policy—as producers step up purchases in expectation of rising consumption demand—but mainly this type of stimulus is expected to come later, after consumer expenditure increases have lifted retail sales, raised production, reduced unemployment and expanded the flow of business and personal income. It is also maintained by the proponents of this approach that the fuller utilization of capacity which they expect to see achieved will, by lowering unit costs of production, make it possible both to reduce prices—which would expand consumers' real income—and to have a higher rate of return on invested capital. The latter, in turn, is expected to promote a larger volume of investment expenditures.

Grounds for skepticism as to the feasibility of lifting and holding employment and production to the desired levels by means of emergency across-the-board tax reduction or by stepped-up rates of federal expenditures have already been stated. So also have the reservations that come to mind as to the fiscal implications, in view of the present and prospective deficit position of the federal budget, of our government's seeking to achieve its employment objectives by these means. It will suffice, therefore, to comment briefly on the possibility, not so frequently proposed nowadays but nonetheless a familiar and widely-held point of view, that the performance of our economy could be improved by a faster rate of increase in money wage rates.

Certainly it cannot be said that we lack experience with this approach to the augmentation of aggregate demand. Wage and salary payments have been rising faster than the real output of our economy for a considerable time, but with no apparent effect other than to put increasing pressure on costs and prices. Since the end of World War II, average hourly compensation in private nonagricultural industries, including supplements to wages and salaries, increased on the average of five percent a year. Increases in direct wage and salary payments and in so-called fringe benefits are the characteristic means by which the material benefits of our economic system are transmitted to the people, but wage and related labor cost increases at a five percent rate, because they exceed productivity improvements by a wide margin, cannot fail but produce a rise in unit cost of production and put an upward pressure on prices. Although it would be an egregious mistake to attribute full responsibility for the price level inflation of recent years to money labor cost increases, we must all the same attribute a considerable part of it to this factor. And the postwar inflation has been considerable. Between 1953 and 1963 gross national product rose by $154 billion in current prices, but by only $89 billion in constant prices, that is, by about half as much. In other words, of the total increase in current price GNP over this period, roughly fifty percent was only a reflection of higher prices. But in recent years, because of the greater resistance to price increases the effect of rapid wage advances has been more to narrow the margin between costs and prices than to raise prices. As stated earlier, this has tended to hold down corporate profits, to suppress the rate of expenditure by business concerns on investment goods, and to hold economic growth to a slow rate. In the present circumstances, a strategy of economic policy which would promote a still higher rate of increase in per-hour wage and salary payments would invite, indeed would almost certainly require, either an accelerated inflation of prices or a still heavier suppression of economic growth, or some of both. Whatever other damage would be caused by an experiment of this kind, it would diminish our capacity to compete in world markets and would make it well-nigh impossible to accomplish —except at the expense of a near-total dismantling of our mutual security program—the improvement in our international balance of payments which is an absolute criterion for the success of any economic strategy at this time. Fortunately, it is a strategy that has few advocates.

* * * *

There is another approach, however. Interest has shifted of late to the possibility of giving our economy the stimulus it needs by means which would in the first instance encourage business concerns to step up their capital expenditures. It is more and more widely recognized that this is the area in which our economy has been lagging. We have, of course, been scoring striking scientific and engineering successes, and private business concerns are currently spending close to $38 billion a year on plant and equipment, but the fact of the matter is that in a period in which spending on capital goods has been increasing by leaps and bounds in other advanced industrial countries of the world, spending of this type in the American economy has increased hardly at all. Private producers' expenditures for plant and equipment in 1962 are currently anticipated to be only slightly higher than they were in 1957, six years ago. And considering the fact that the cost of factory construction and the prices of industrial equipment have increased significantly in that time, these figures tell us that we are currently putting in place a smaller volume of physical facilities and equipment than we were installing six years ago. That a step-up in capital expenditures would be stimulative in the short-term cyclical situation is contested by no one. But more than that, it is clear that over the long run it is impossible significantly to improve our capability for achieving a higher rate of growth without expanding and improving the base of our productive facilities. If there is a lag in our economy, this is it.

It would be wrong in seeking to find an explanation for this lethargy in capital goods spending to give attention only to the trend of corporate profits, but it is certainly pertinent to observe that the aggregate of corporate profits after taxes in 1962 has been only very little higher than in 1959 and has shown relatively little increase in the last seven years. And, reflecting the fact that corporate dividends have been lifted in the aggregate since 1950 in about the same proportion as total personal income, corporate retained income has shown no upward trend at all in the post-Korean conflict period. Clearly, an effective strategy of economic policy at this time must somehow improve the profit performance of American business and, through this means, end the lag in business investment expenditures.

Having this need in mind, and considering also the fiscal and other constraints under which we must operate at this time, let me turn to the major features of what would be an appropriate economic strategy.

*   *   *   *

Our most pressing present need is for changes in the rates and methods of taxation that will carry the highest potentiality for stimulating increased private investment expenditures. Important steps have already been taken to this end. The liberalization of depreciation allowances introduced in mid-1962 was a useful move in this direction. Although it does not reduce the tax load, and does not improve the rate of return to capital over the full life of the investment goods involved, it does afford taxpayers a more liberal opportunity to defer taxes while invested capital is being recouped. Also, the investment credit provision enacted in 1962, which permits an actual reduction in the tax burden in eligible cases of equipment purchases, should have a stimulative effect on capital goods expenditures.

But even taken together, these steps cannot be regarded as providing all that is needed. A program designed to stimulate a higher level of capital expenditures by business must first provide for a direct reduction in corporate income tax rates, allowing, for a time at least, an increase in the rate of return to invested capital and an enlargement in the flow of funds available for financing an expansion of corporate assets.

I say "for a time at least" because, although a corporate tax rate reduction would improve rates of return to capital as an immediate effect, and would be an incentive to increased investment, this effect would not be permanent. Studies of the shifting and incidence of corporate income taxes suggest that lower rates would lead to some lowering of prices and that the returns to invested capital would, as these price adjustments were made, be reduced to earlier levels. But this is no fault in the proposal; indeed, it makes it doubly desirable. It means that a cut in corporate income tax rates would initially provide a stimulus to investment expenditures, creating jobs in the process, and would later be transformed into a stimulus to consumption.

The expansive effect of corporate income tax reduction on capital spending would be partly aborted to the extent that the increment to after-tax corporate income was disbursed in dividends rather than retained by the companies. Some increase in dividend payments should be anticipated, but studies of corporate financial behavior show that in the short run dividend payments move relatively slowly as compared with the amount of after-tax income retained in the business and it is reasonable to expect, therefore, that for the period of time in which the stimulus to investment goods expenditure is most needed the major impact of a corporate tax reduction would be to increase both the incentive to private investment spending and the means for its financing.

Second, a tax program designed to promote a higher level of business investment expenditures should also permit of a reduction in the current near-confiscatory rates of taxation on the upper brackets of personal income and, to the extent possible, on the very high rates imposed on income in the intermediate brackets. Such a move would make investments funds, especially equity investment funds, both more generally available and less costly, would give strong encouragement to enterprises of the more venturesome type, and would greatly enhance incentives for the entrepreneurial and risk-taking individuals who provide much of the drive in our economy.

Quite apart from its beneficial impact on the large companies that provide the bulk of employment in our economy, a joint program of this type would give long-needed help to our country's numerous small and medium-sized business concerns, a substantial part of whose net earnings are absorbed every year in federal income taxes. Having served for four years as Chairman of President Eisenhower's Cabinet Committee on Small Business, let me say that in my judgment this is the most effective and genuinely constructive way open to us for assisting small business. We can supplement this by such measures as loans, assistance in obtaining procurement contracts, help in gaining access to research results, etc., but nothing can take the place of a reduction in the tax burden as a way to help small business. And it is vitally important that we give effective and constructive assistance to these concerns. The task we face in the remainder of this decade of providing jobs for a rapidly increasing number of young people will require a vigorous community of small businesses as well as prosperous, rapidly-growing large companies.

*   *   *   *

I need not tell you that it would be tremendously agreeable to be able to go beyond these two steps to a reduction of tax rates on the lower brackets of personal income. But we must, in my judgment, reconcile ourselves to the fact that in our present fiscal situation all our heart's desires for a lessening of the tax burden cannot be accomplished at one time and in one year. Certainly it cannot be done without broadly parallel reductions in government expenditures, that is, in government activities. But for such reductions there is little or no support. There is, undoubtedly, some unreasoned feeling nowadays that we can have both lower taxes at all levels and more government, but this is not a workable formula. There is a point at which less taxation means less government. My estimate of the situation is that although many are anxious for the first, few are ready for the second. What we need to do at this time, therefore, is to make a beginning in tax reduction which will be within our fiscal capability and which will give the most stimulus to the economy for the least revenue loss.

The steps I have suggested would be such a beginning. They would give a considerable stimulus to the economy and they could be made at a relatively modest cost; they should be regarded as the first phase of a program which, if the uptrend in federal spending is held in check, could subsequently be extended and broadened. A reduction of the corporate income tax rate to the 42 percent proposed in the Baker-Herlong bill would be very helpful, but a reduction to 47 percent, that is, by five percentage points, could properly be set as an interim goal. Its revenue-loss impact would be about $2½ billion for a full fiscal year. And significant reduction of personal income tax rates could be afforded with a relatively small revenue loss, say of $1½ billion. The important point is that to hold the annual cost of tax reduction to figures of this magnitude would keep the program within fiscally manageable limits. It would mean that the reductions could be financed out of the normal increment to federal revenues from economic growth, which is about $3 to $4 billion a year. We would satisfy the first requirement that should be imposed on fiscal policy today, namely, that it should contemplate no increase in our present budgetary deficit but, as soon as possible, should permit a decrease.

*   *   *   *

It is clear, of course, that a tax reduction of $3 to $4 billion would pre-empt the full increase in revenue-gathering capability that can be expected from economic growth. And it follows from this that it would leave no room for a concurrent increase in spending without inviting an almost certain enlargement of the present deficit. Yet some increase in federal spending is inevitable. Defense requirements are almost certain to be increased as a result of the establishment by the Russians of a full-scale military base in the Caribbean. And we have only recently entered into a program looking to the landing of manned vehicles on the moon. Interest costs on the federal debt are more likely to rise than to fall. And there are many civilian programs of government that need additional support as well as others that are going to be more costly whether we wish it or not. How can we manage, then, to have both lower taxes and increased expenditures?

It is no answer to this question to say that we will just have a larger deficit, and that it will somehow come out all right in the end. This would be less a program than a gamble. And it is not necessary to take this gamble. The fact is that it is possible to fund, that is to finance, additional expenditure on needed programs in good part out of reductions in expenditure on programs that are either entirely indefensible or, while defensible in principle, have been carried too far. Let me turn to a consideration of these possibilities.

There are three approaches on which I shall comment: two —the blocking of loopholes in tax laws and the reduction of expenditures—are well-known; the third—the sale of financial assets held by federal agencies—is less familiar, though in the present situation it has certain unique advantages. Let us consider these in the order named.

Whatever the merits on grounds of equity of closing loopholes, most such changes would have a retarding effect on investment, which is a powerful drawback to their use in a situation in which our leading objective is to stimulate a higher level of investment. For example, whatever one may think of the merits, on grounds of equity or in any other sense, of liberal oil, gas and mineral depletion allowances, one would expect a reduction of these allowances to retard exploratory and developmental expenditures in mining operations. Again, equity aside, it must be conceded that to treat as income for tax purposes a part of the proceeds from the sale of real estate currently treated for tax purposes as capital gains would discourage investment in real estate properties and almost certainly would suppress new construction expenditures. And, third, whatever one may think of stock options as a way of rewarding corporate personnel, if compensation to corporate officers in the form of stock options and other nonsalary emoluments are important to incentive, as they doubtless are, a substantial reduction in the after-tax value of these benefits could have a significantly restrictive effect on enterprise. In short, the correction of an inequity, even an egregious one, can be restrictive in its economic effect.

Attempting to fund tax revenue losses through loophole closing has a second serious drawback in the present situation.

Tax changes of this type inevitably involve long and hard-fought legislative struggles and could delay for months, with uncertain outcome, the launching of tax relief measures. The fact is, however, that tax relief measures are needed as soon as possible. Without prejudice to the possibility of ultimately correcting inequitable features of our tax laws, an attempt to fund tax reduction revenue losses by this method in the 1962–63 context would have to be regarded, on grounds of timing, as ill-advised.

*   *   *   *

But loophole closing is not the only means by which to fund the revenue losses that will inevitably result from tax reduction. There are significant opportunities to accomplish this through expenditure reductions that will have no negative impact on the level of production, employment or income. Regrettably, there is much defeatism on the possibility of expenditure reduction—a state of mind that arises from the fact that the budget is so large and its management is such a distant and obscure process to the great majority of our citizens that there is a temptation to assume that nothing can be done about it. But the fact is that a good deal can be done about it.

Consider the following possibilities. First, new commitments for direct loans by the federal government are estimated to total nearly $3 billion more in fiscal 1963 than in fiscal 1961. In two years alone, direct lending under federal credit programs has increased from an annual rate of $5 billion to $8 billion. Within this total are programs that range all the way from mortgage purchases by the Federal National Mortgage Association to loans made by the Agency for International Development. Only the difference between the disbursements made under these loan commitments in a given fiscal year and the repayments received in that year on loans made in earlier years is a burden on the federal budget. But the budget submitted in January, 1962 estimated the burden for fiscal 1963 at $1.8 billion. Thus, an overall reduction of ten percent in total disbursements would yield a budget saving of $800 million, or nearly fifty percent of the current budget cost of the programs. And in view of the fact that interest rate adjustments would make it possible for much of this lending activity to be conducted through private financial agencies, no reduction of overall investment activity would necessarily result. This is one of the most promising areas that can be found for federal spending reductions that need have no net negative effect, even in the short run, on the total volume of spending in the economy.

Second, federal expenditures for public works, civil and military combined, increased by $500 million between fiscal 1961 and fiscal 1962 and are estimated to increase by an additional $700 million in fiscal 1963. A return in fiscal 1964 to the fiscal 1962 rate, which would be accomplished by a relatively minor rescheduling of existing projects, would provide a saving of nearly $200 to $250 million annually.

Third, the application of reasonable standards of user charges under a number of federal programs provides additional opportunities for net expenditure reduction.

There are other areas in which expenditure reductions would be justified but in which there is little hope, for the moment at least, of making changes. A reduction, for example, in the tremendous cost of our programs of assistance to agriculture, which were estimated at $6 billion in fiscal 1962, an increase of $1 billion over expenditures in the previous fiscal year, waits upon the enactment by the Congress of a program under which gradual downward adjustments can be made in price supports and parallel relaxations effected in production controls. It is impractical, however, to count on such changes to help fund a 1963 tax reduction program.

How practical, on the other hand, are the suggestions I have made? It may be maintained that economies of the character and magnitude of those I have suggested—they would approach two billion dollars—could not be accomplished, despite the fact that in considerable part they could be carried out without additional legislation. It may be argued, for example, that loan programs are inadequate at present, and should be extended to additional areas; that public construction should be accelerated, well above its present level; and that user charges should be reduced, not extended and increased.

Maybe so, but if that is the case, and if the prospect before us is for a continuation of expenditure increases of the order of $5 to $6 billion annually, which is the current rate of increase, then our hope for noninflationary tax reduction is clearly illusory. If this is our fiscal outlook, responsible fiscal policy will have to turn to a search for additional sources of federal revenue. The outlook would be for an increase in the tax burden, not a decrease.

Let me state, again, the imperative which I see in our present fiscal situation and to which our economic strategy must be accommodated. At present, federal expenditures are increasing at a rate—$5 to $6 billion a year—that exceeds by as much as $1 to $2 billion a year the rate at which we can expect tax revenues to rise even when our economy is operating at full tilt. Accordingly, since we begin from a deficit position—nearly $8 billion in fiscal 1963—expenditure control and reduction is an absolute essential if tax reduction is to be carried out without substantially enlarging the present budgetary deficit.

*   *   *   *

Let me turn briefly to the third possible source for funding, in this case temporarily, the budgetary effect of tax reduction or expenditure increase. This can be done by the sale of some part of the stock of financial assets currently held by the federal government.

It is not widely recognized what a vast stockpile of financial assets the federal government has accumulated over the years. The Budget Message of January, 1962 estimated that these holdings would come close to $29 billion by the end of fiscal 1963. As examples of the types of financial assets involved, it is estimated that there will be $3.7 billion of mortgage holdings of the Federal National Mortgage Association, $1.8 billion of the obligations of local governments held by the Community Facilities Administration of the Housing and Home Finance Agency, $1.9 billion of home mortgages held by the Veterans' Administration, and $3.3 billion of business loans held by the Export-Import Bank.

There would be no novelty in the sale to the public of parts of these federally-held financial assets. The concept of a secondary market agency such as the Federal National Mortgage Association contemplates the sale of assets as well as their purchase. And home mortgages have been sold by FNMA, as well as by VA. Only recently, a program was inaugurated under which loans of the Export-Import Bank were sold abroad. And assets of the Home Owners' Loan Corporation were liquidated in the 1940's and those of the Reconstruction Finance Corporation in 1953.

It would be necessary, of course, to schedule sales with an eye to their effect on the long-term capital market and thus on the economy; obviously, sales would have to be made on a basis that would be fully protective of the public interest. In both of these matters, much would depend on the timing and volume of the sales, and on how they were made. Various methods of sale could be used. One would be to offer to the public a type of collateral receipt representing an interest in a body of federally-held securities. Because many of the financial assets currently held by the Treasury are loans that were made at below-market interest rates, the Treasury would probably be able to recoup less than the par value of the original securities or loans. But this would depend on the type of security sold to the public, principally on whether it carried tax exemption and whether guaranteed by the federal government. The more attractive the tax and guarantee features of the security offered, the less likely, of course, that sales would have to be made at prices below par.

But even if less than par value was recovered, an actual loss to the federal government would not necessarily be indicated when all costs and returns are netted out. For the Treasury to hold financial assets involves a continuing cost to the federal government of the difference between the income earned on them and the cost of borrowing public debt funds in order to continue holding them. The total of these annual differences, each discounted to the present at relevant interest rates, represents the present value of the annual costs involved in holding the assets over their expected lives. Against this calculated cost, which would be saved if the assets were sold, one would balance such capital loss as might be involved in their sale. Whether there would be, on balance, a net loss or cost to the federal government would depend principally on the relation between these two capital values. But even if a loss were involved, it should be regarded as a means, fortunately not requiring current out-of-pocket expenditure, of funding a subsidy once and for all.

Naturally, the amount and timing of such financial asset sales should be scheduled with a view to the state of the economy and the capital markets. At this point a question of harmonization of monetary policy with fiscal policy arises. Considering the need for a generally expansionist economic policy, the current need is for a monetary policy which will promote the greatest availability of credit and the lowest level of interest rates consistent with our balance of payments situation. A program of financial asset sales would tend to raise long-term interest rates. Although it would not collide with balance of payments requirements, it might require support from monetary policy if it were to be effective in helping to fund tax reductions without being restrictive of economic growth. However, there is a relative surplus of funds available for investment in the capital market at this time and, if anything, a lack of adequate financial instruments in which to invest them. It is not likely, therefore, that a properly scheduled sales program would unduly affect the level or structure of interest rates and borrowing costs. If this were to happen, it would be necessary and desirable to have support from the Federal Reserve System to enable the assets to be shifted from public to private ownership without a restrictive capital market impact.

Between the reduction of net expenditures in selected federal programs and financial asset sales, on the one hand, and the normal growth of federal revenues from expanding production and income, on the other, it should be possible in the second half of fiscal 1963 and in fiscal 1964 to have a $4 billion (annual rate) tax reduction program and a significant increase in selected expenditure programs without even the two combined contributing to an immediate increase in budgetary deficits. Additional tax reductions in future fiscal periods, and the elimination of current deficits, would depend on the rate of growth of the economy, on our success in resisting increases in federal expenditures, and the possible continuation of some asset sales. While the possibilities of funding such a fiscal program through selective expenditure reduction and by financial asset sales are by no means inexhaustible, they would not be exhausted in eighteen months and, if the improvement in the rate of economic growth and in business profits are good, as they should be, the elimination of budgetary deficits concurrently with additional tax reductions would come quickly enough. Deficits of the size we now have cannot be eliminated at once. But they should not be increased, and we can and should lay out a strategy that projects realistically their eventual elimination. This I have sought to do.

*   *   *   *

In judging the merits of this strategy on economic grounds I think we would want to insist on three points having to do with the harmonization, as it were, of economic policies, private as well as public. First, it would be futile to attempt to stimulate our economy through tax reduction and, concurrently, to retard it with an unduly restrictive money policy. Clearly, in the present context we need just as liberal a monetary policy as our balance of payments will permit.

Second, the more progress that can be made in redressing the imbalance in our international payments, the more aggressively we can use monetary policy as a means of lifting our economy's growth rate. This is not the place to launch into a discussion of ways and means for correcting the imbalance in international accounts. It must suffice to point out that progress, and real progress, in this area of our performance is absolutely essential to a solution of our domestic growth problem that is consistent with our international obligations.

Third, any success we might have in lifting the profit squeeze by an alleviation of the tax burden could be cancelled by unit production cost increases originating elsewhere. Because the chief potential source of such cost increases would be labor cost advances substantially in excess of productivity improvements, it follows that appropriate wage and related policies are absolutely essential if we are to avoid undoing by excessive labor cost increases all the good that tax reduction can accomplish.

This is obviously what the President had in mind in setting forth certain wage and price guidelines in his January, 1962 Economic Report. I fear, however, that the wage guideline expressed there is not fully suited to the present situation. What is needed now is a chance to achieve an improvement in profit margins and some reduction in prices. This requires that production cost increases be kept *well within* productivity improvements, not that they be made *equivalent to* productivity improvements and the statement of guidelines should be revised to this end.

Furthermore, important questions remain as to how best to achieve a result conforming to a stated guideline without intruding unduly into the procedures of free collective bargaining. In this connection I should like to restate certain proposals I have already made to the Joint Economic Committee.

First, I would suggest that the Executive branch limit its role in wage-price-profit matters to the preparation of an annual review, presented in the year-end Economic Report of the Council of Economic Advisers, of major developments affecting wages, prices and profits and to the presentation by the President, in his year-end Economic Message, of an evaluation of the wage-price-profit developments of the year.[1] There is ample opportunity there for the President to state whether, in his judgment, wage and other cost developments have been inconsistent with the national interest and, if this is the case, for him to make proposals for such adjustments as are needed.

Second, in the meantime, efforts should be pressed to explore ways of improving the balance of bargaining power in labor-management relations, a critical matter that has been under examination by the President's special Commission on Labor-Management Relations, though as yet without publicly disclosed results.

Third, a better understanding among labor, management

---

1. Strangely enough, treatment of the wage-price-profit question and of the so-called guidelines in the January, 1963 Report of CEA was cursory, at best, and to all intents and purposes the President added nothing to what he had already said.

and government on the sensitive issues involved in wage-price-profit relationships is aided by conferences such as the one on national economic issues sponsored in the spring of 1962 by the Secretary of Labor. These should be held regularly, at least once a year, and timed to have maximum impact on policy formation in the Executive branch as well as in the Congress.

Fourth, it would be helpful to reactivate the Committee on Government Activities Affecting Costs and Prices which was established in 1959 and which has since been disbanded. This committee, if it had the full cooperation of all the executive departments and agencies concerned, could help avoid the many ways in which government, through its own activities, inflates costs or abets their inflation and puts the kind of pressure on cost-price relationships that tends to suppress our rate of economic growth.

Fifth, it would be helpful if the Joint Economic Committee, in connection with its annual review of the Economic Message of the President, would make a particular point of taking testimony from all those with useful contributions to make to the discussion of wage-price-profit policies. Hearings devoted specifically to this purpose might help us find a route to the kind of wage-price policy, shaped through free collective bargaining and competitive markets, under which we can achieve an improved economic performance. It would also help consolidate public opinion behind appropriate public and private policies.

*   *   *   *

Finally, let me comment on the question whether there is a need for additional administrative machinery for shaping and carrying out our federal economic policy. Two suggestions occur to me at once. One has been mentioned, namely, to reactivate the interdepartmental Committee on Government Activities Affecting Costs and Prices. A second would be to establish a group that would follow continuously and make recommendation on the conduct of federal credit programs. In 1956–60 this was done as an activity of the Advisory Board on Economic Growth and Stability under the Chairman of the Council of Economic Advisers. But ABEGS was disbanded in 1961; so also, so far as is publicly known, was the regular conference on credit program policies. In view of the immense size and complexity of these credit operations, provision should be made for regular inter-agency discussions looking to the coordination of policy. These two suggestions may seem like very modest ones, but let me say quite confidently that they are not. On the contrary, they are absolutely brimming with potentialities for good, and for controversy, too.

For reasons that I do not altogether understand, interest in the creation of new policy-making machinery has ignored possibilities such as these two in favor of devices for coordinating economic policy at the Cabinet level and especially for harmonizing monetary policy with the other major arms of economic policy. There may be useful innovations to be made in this connection, but whatever is eventually done, let no one believe that there is any present shortage of ways and means for harmonizing economic and financial policy. The possibility of close cooperation between the Treasury and the Federal Reserve Board has been fully demonstrated for years. The same has been true of relations between the Council of Economic Advisers and the Federal Reserve Board. In addition, regular weekly meetings of the Cabinet and of the Advisory Board on Economic Growth and Stability (with the membership of the latter including one of the governors of the Federal Reserve Board and the Under Secretary or parallel officer of each department and agency of the Executive branch having a major economic mission) provided two forums during the Eisenhower administration for extended discussion of economic policy questions. Still another forum was created with the establishment in 1957 of an *ad hoc* monetary and financial policy committee headed by the President and including the Secretary of the Treasury, the Chairman of the Board of Governors of the Federal Reserve System, the Chairman of the Council of Economic Advisers, and the Special Assistant to the President for Economic Affairs. To these resources for the discussion of policy questions must be added, of course, the countless occasions in the daily business of government that keep policy-making officials in close and constant contact with one another, and which provide all the opportunity needed for exchange of views.

Thus, within the framework of arrangements that have been shown to be workable, there are adequate facilities for the shaping and coordination of policy and no lack of opportunity for any cognizant agency to know the thinking of others. This is not to say that different observers of economic and financial developments, even when they understand one another's minds perfectly, will at all times see policy needs in exactly the same manner. But no conceivable design of governmental machinery will guarantee this. If an addition is to be made to the formidable array of machinery already available, it would be to provide for a continuing Economic and Financial Council of Cabinet-level officers. Such a Council should include the Chairman of the Board of Governors of the Federal Reserve System when agenda items warranting his attention are involved, but not otherwise. It would provide for Cabinet-level discussion of economic matters at lengths not always feasible in regular cabinet meetings, paralleling in economics and finance the work of the National Security Council in its area. Membership should be limited to Cabinet-rank officers with a major economic mission, but it would be useful to include, in addition to the Federal Reserve Chairman, the heads of certain of the major federal lending agencies, such as the Housing and Home Finance Agency and the Export-Import Bank, and the heads of federal agencies having major administrative responsibilities in economic and financial matters, such as the Agency for International Development. Secretariat responsibilities for the Council should be provided by the Council of Economic Advisers and the Chairman of the Council, who should of course be one of the Council's members, should have responsibility for the preparation and documentation of the Council's agenda and for the presentation of agenda items at Council meetings under the President's chairmanship.

Proposals to improve the performance of our economy by changing the machinery of government for policy formulation more often reveal a poverty of ideas than any special depth of understanding of governmental operations. But the Cabinet-level Council suggested here, and which in one form or another has been previously proposed by others, could be quite helpful. And the two other suggestions I have made would fill real gaps in our present arrangements.

*   *   *   *

I have concentrated in these policy suggestions on the major economic and financial problems confronting our country at this time. The central problem is how to improve our economic performance through the first installment of a selective tax restructuring and tax reduction program, and how to do this in ways consistent with the correction of our two major financial imbalances, namely, the large deficits in our balance of international payments and in federal budgetary transactions.

I would not claim for the strategy I have sketched that it will eliminate the budgetary deficit on as fast a schedule as we might like. I would claim, however, that, while helping us to achieve a better level of production, employment and income, the policy approach proposed here will not deepen the fiscal imbalance and should, over a reasonable period of time, lead to its correction. What is needed at this point is not a sudden solution to a problem that threatens to be chronic. What we need to do is to set ourselves onto a course which will give some assurance of carrying us eventually to budgetary balance. What is needed is a strategy that will show some light at the end of a tunnel which, at this writing, is dark for as far as we can see.

There are, of course, many additional areas of policy in which supporting actions would help improve the performance of our economy and help advance our national purpose. I have repeatedly referred to the need to correct the deficit in our balance of international payments as a means, among other things, for releasing monetary policy from the constraints under which it currently works. Aggressive efforts to this end must be continued. In addition, we must never relax our efforts to keep our economy constructively competitive. We must never, of course, cease in our efforts to correct maladjustments of resource allocation, such as those that in agriculture are nowadays placing fabulous and apparently never-ending burdens on our federal budget. And I am sure I need not say to this audience that the reduction of unemployment will require even greater efforts in the future than in the past to improve the level of educational achievement of those whose employment opportunities are least favorable. There is no single factor more deeply involved in the distressing problem of unemployment than inadequate educational accomplishment. This is partly a problem of physical facilities and instructional staff, and it is partly a problem of motivation. We must find answers to all three.

Supplemented along these and still other lines, the broad approach to fiscal policy which I have sketched will give us our best chance for achieving the central objective of the Employment Act, namely, an adequate expansion of employment opportunities and through this the improvement of individual and family well-being which is our specific economic goal. But I have been at particular pains to propose an approach which will not only help us reach these purely economic objectives but will, in the process, help strengthen our system of private competitive enterprise and our democratic political institutions. As such, it affords us, also, our best chance for achieving our paramount national purpose: maximum opportunities for self-directed personal development and fulfillment in an environment of freedom.